The
Best of Friends

The Best of Friends

John Aspinall

HARPER & ROW, PUBLISHERS
New York, Hagerstown, San Francisco, London

FIRST U.S. EDITION

ISBN: 0-06-010153-9

LIBRARY OF CONGRESS CATALOG CARD NUMBER: 76-26211

77 78 79 80 81 10 9 8 7 6 5 4 3 2 1

Contents

Acknowledgements

I WOULD like to thank all those who have helped to create Howletts. The constant love and support of my mother from my earliest years has provided me with a 'fall back' area, without which I would probably never have found the courage to succeed in life at all. My wife, Sally, has never wavered in her confidence and trust, and without her backing, emotional and otherwise, I doubt whether I could have survived the recent difficult years. The loyalty and enthusiasm of my half-brother, James Osborne, and his wife, Janie, have been another prop in the difficult years of transition from a private to public zoo. My hopes for the future of Howletts and Port Lympne rest on my three children, Jamunda, Damian and Bassa, who I trust will dedicate their abilities to protecting the remnants of wild nature wherever they find them, and help the breeding colonies that I built up coast into the third millennium.

I must render thanks also to Mrs Dorothy Hastings and her mother, the late Mrs Trevenon Coode, for their work in the late fifties looking after Gugis, Shamba, Baby Doll and the other gorillas when they were babies. Also to Beryl Addley who has looked after my children for the past twelve years undeterred by the presence of baby gorillas, tiger cubs, wolf puppies and wild boar squeakers in her nursery.

Not to be forgotten are the 'keeper pioneers' of Howletts – Kurt Paulich, Brian Stocks and Nick Marx are surely the best and bravest big cat keepers in the world. Richard Johnstone-Scott and his assistant Peter Halliday with their apes and monkeys are men of the same calibre. A word must be said here for the elephant keeper, Paul Ottley. He has agreed to work out his life with the elephants and when the four resident bulls reach adulthood he is prepared to face the necessary risks to get a birth. A lesser interval, we hope, awaits Jimmy Shave, the black rhino keeper. He expects a birth within thirty months from Baringo and Rukwa. Contrasted with the great personal bravery of the Howletts keepers is their gentleness in the hand-rearing of rejected infants. My gratitude also to Tom Begg, the resident veterinary surgeon, for the dedicated application of his specialised skills during the last three years.

A special word must be said for my secretary and confidante, Susan Hunt, who has been with me for eight years. She has lived with this book from its earliest stages, typing out my difficult longhand and keeping me up to the mark. My thanks also to Nicholas Gould for the revision and correction of my manuscript.

I will not forget the support afforded me in the new Port Lympne Wildlife Sanctuary project by my old friends Alan Clore, Simon Fraser, Jim Slater, Gordon White and Selim Zilkha, all of whom answered the call when it came.

Finally, always in my mind are my great friends, Edward and James Goldsmith and Lord Londonderry, whose unwavering support, moral and financial, has helped make Howletts, let alone this book, possible.

John Aspinall

Introduction

IT is hard for me to say truthfully when my regard for animals began. My interest was certainly aroused at a very early period of my life. Like many of the generations of my family before me, I was born in India, or rather in what is now called Pakistan, and I can recollect that a great friend of my mother's, Tony Benyon, had two half-grown tigers which he kept on a lead. I was four or five at the time and this clearly added to 'Uncle Tony's' prestige in my eyes. My mother's uncle by marriage, Stewart Ross, at one time owned a pair of adult elephant cows, Muni and Rada. I can vividly remember feeding them with sugar-cane and then being lifted high in their trunks and settled back on the ground without being hurt. Even then I was awed by their power and gentleness.

When I went to private school in Eastbourne, at the age of seven, I spent some of my holidays on a farm in Sussex, as my parents were in India. I was fortunate enough to come under the influence of the farmer, Jack Pring. I stayed with the Prings for many years until I was thirteen or more and in many respects Jack Pring acted towards me as a surrogate father. Palfrey Farm of a hundred-odd acres was part of the great Petworth property and had been in the ownership of the Wyndham family for centuries. The fields were ancient and small, and the surrounding country wild and beautiful with much oak forest and abandoned common land. Mr Pring was of the old school of stock-farmer. All the eighteen milch cows had names and all were milked by hand. A hybrid Guernsey bull by the name of John stood resident in the barn. He was feared and respected by all, as indeed was Esau, the large, white boar. I worked on a friendship with Esau until he would allow me, and me alone, to ride on his back. The greatest excitement would be when he would wander into the fearsome stinging-nettle clumps. I loved his smell and his brittle temper and the feeling of safety by association that he gave me. I relished also the satisfaction that comes from a friendship with an animal feared by others. To Jack Pring each animal was a character and a personality. Even some of the hens and geese had names and characteristics.

The impressions from Palfrey Farm have remained with me always. The saddest day was market day when some animals had to be disposed of for cash, a commodity which seemed always to be in short supply, the shortage of which was the very reason I was staying there in the first place, as Mrs Pring took in children during holidays for a small fee. The farmhouse was Elizabethan and almost untouched by the passage of time. There was no electric light or power of any sort. In those days a farm of this nature was almost self-supporting. The Prings made their own butter and cured their own hams in a chimney vault large enough to hang a horse. Warmth came not only from the huge log fire which was never allowed to die during the winter months, but from the organic affection bestowed upon us by the Pring family, father, mother and daughters. Father Pring was a patriarch and, by his example, encouraged manliness and adventure, accompanied as it must be by periods of discomfort. Though thoughtful of his domestic charges, he waged a constant war against certain animals which he regarded as time-honoured competitors. Foxes, rabbits and woodpigeons bore the brunt of this historic misunderstanding. However, the intelligence of the former and the reproductive resilience of the latter ensured that the conflict was a perennial one. The culture of the country classes at that period decreed that certain creatures were either cultivated for the pleasure of live target practice or were vermin to be exterminated. There was also a third and neutral category which included birds that were rare or inedible, or by some strange fancy had entered the folklore of the people. When I was given a catapult at the age of nine or ten, I was told that I could hunt starlings and sparrows but was on no account to molest thrushes, blackbirds or robins. Squirrels, rats and rabbits were fair game for a small boy with a bow and later a Diana air-gun. As I matured, these weapons were replaced progressively by a four-ten, sixteen-bore and finally twelve-bore shot-gun. It was not until I was twenty-three or four that I threw aside these weapons and decided that I must disregard the whole concept of a war against certain categories of mammal and bird.

By some strange process the ritualised destruction of harmless and often beautiful species of bird and mammal had become equated with manliness and virility. A weird left-over of our half-baked hunting impulse, it had led the governing classes of the countryside and their imitators into a cold spiritual void from which they find it difficult, even today, to extricate themselves. It was years before I realised the *cul-de-sac* of field sports was not for me. From Farmer Pring I learned the fellowship of mammals, from my step-father, Sir George Osborne, I learned respect for plants, countryside and people. Looking back on my memory of him I am amazed how a man of such warmth and honour, with a genuine love of the countryside, could have spent so many mornings and afternoons killing defenceless birds and mammals. The fact that so many of the old ruling elite became de-culturalised in this fashion may even be partly responsible for their terminal decline. Even today, if ten per cent of the cash and commitment put into the organisation of mass battues was diverted to the protection of indigenous plants and animals, the situation would be markedly changed for the better.

When I was eleven years old, I became the owner of a large dappled polecat ferret. We went rabbit-hunting together and after a year he escaped to be replaced by the first of several jackdaws. One of these birds stayed with me for over two years. When I went to Rugby School I managed to take my jackdaw with me. The fact that he could recognise me from five hundred yards high in the sky and fly down and perch on my shoulders, made me inordinately proud. On one occasion, on a summer afternoon, he landed on my shoulder when I was batting for the school. Eventually he drowned himself in a water-butt. My friendship with the half-wild ferrets and the young jackdaws stirred something deep within me, some response that was not elicited by my relationship with the numerous dogs that shared my step-father's home at Framfield in Sussex. I liked dogs and cats but they did not stir my imagination. It is difficult to be uplifted by a Dalmatian or a budgerigar. I needed the tinge of unpredictability, of independence, to invite my full respect. Without wildness there can be no ingredient of fear and without fear, even fear of a nip from a ferret, or a peck from a jackdaw, there must be a lessening of respect. Of course, a dog, cat or horse may bite, scratch or kick, but this is considered an aberration in animals that have suffered thousands of years of guided selective breeding – a process that is intended to reduce them to obedience or, in the case of the cat, compliance.

During my three years in the Royal Marines and those that followed at Oxford, little was to be discerned of my love of nature. In the Marines I read

the poets; at Oxford I felt, for the first time, the cards in my hand. There I became a gambler, 'a notorious plunger' as Paul Johnson once described me in the *New Statesman*. From inauspicious beginnings in a modest poker school at Oriel College, after many vicissitudes, grew a fortune large enough to enable me to befriend and breed wild animals on the scale of Howletts and Port Lympne. All that is another story, but worth the telling, as to this day 'gambler's gold' is the coinage that feeds the beasts, pays the wages and foots the mounting bills.

What was it that made me buy a Capuchin monkey and a tigress the moment that I had sufficient money to support them, and then two Himalayan bears? As an incurable romantic, I know what I would like to think but the faint streak of realism that has always just kept me within bounds, precludes me from giving a satisfactory answer.

In 1956, following a considerable win on Prelone in the Cesarewitch Handicap at Newmarket, I purchased Howletts, near Canterbury. The house was built by Sir John Leach in 1787 for an East India Nabob, Isaac Baugh. On his death it was acquired by Sir Thomas Deering, a famous gamester, who lost the whole estate one evening at a game of faro at White's Club. It passed, unsurprisingly, to a money-lender by the name of Abraham Gipps, whose heirs founded Martin's Bank. It is a pure example of the neo-Palladian revival of the time and was restored to its eighteenth-century condition by Philip Jebb and John Fowler. The gardens were redesigned by Russell Page around the remarkable Spanish chestnuts, cedars of Lebanon and ilex trees which have been a feature of the park for centuries.

Howletts made it possible for me to start forming self-perpetuating colonies of wild animals. Numbers grew by birth and acquisition as the years went by. From time to time new enclosures have been made, the most important of which is the gorillarium which houses the sixteen-strong gorilla band.

About six or seven years ago I knew that Howletts, with its mere fifty acres, could not long contain the growing colonies of wild animals. Also at that time I realised that I could not support, indefinitely, the animals from my own diminishing resources. I decided to sell the gaming club in London at the first opportunity, to find a suitable stretch of Kentish parkland near Howletts and open a sanctuary to the public on whom I hoped to defray some of my mounting costs. My first attempt, at Chilham Park, was a failure. Chilham village council, backed by the rural district council and the county authorities, combined against me. We lost the decision at a public enquiry and it was five years before I could find somewhere else and gain planning consent. This I

Port Lympne Wildlife Sanctuary

finally managed to do at Port Lympne, a beautiful estate overlooking the English channel near Folkestone, famous for its gardens and the mansion built in 1912 for Sir Philip Sassoon. By now the relevant authorities had decided that I was no safari-park entrepreneur or circus impresario. Permission was granted and Port Lympne Wildlife Sanctuary and Gardens opened to the public in the early summer of 1976. Sheikh Zayed of Abu Dhabi visited Howletts on 15 September 1974 and promised financial support but after confirming the offer in Abu Dhabi, changed his mind. Help arrived, however, in the confidence and understanding of old friends who knew what I was trying to do and enough money was raised to float the project.

Howletts itself is now open to everyone for eight months of the year from 1 March to 31 October, while Port Lympne is available the whole year round. Already, herds of wild horses, African and Indian buffalo, American bison and Indian deer and antelope have made the move to Port Lympne where there are three hundred acres for them to disport themselves. During 1976, the black rhino, the timber wolves, wild boar and spotted leopards will be shunted across the eighteen miles that separate the two parks. Moving the elephants will be the most exacting task. They will eventually have six acres of grassland and a one-acre yard of hard standing. I invite readers to visit us if they find themselves in the south-east of England and assure themselves of the authenticity of this book.

It is strange that, as I approach my fiftieth year, I have made no record of my life with wild beasts, other than those televised ephemera that please for the moment and then pass for ever. The inhibiting factors have been my own indolence allied to a plenitude of funds, and also, perhaps, a capacity and willingness to talk to anyone who will listen, which has enabled me to find expression without the need to write. Now, however, the fates have conspired to force my hand – towards the pen. The great crash of 1974 has savaged my fortune and crippled my ability to fund a private collection of wild animals which has now bred itself into a horde of 350. If this book is widely read, the revenue from it could amount to a month's feed for the animals at Howletts and Port Lympne. If it fails, my publishers will lose their most generous advance payment – but it will have been swallowed in the throats of rare and hungry beasts, which I am sure will be some consolation to them.

Gorillas

THOSE who know the gorilla well, and they are but few, cannot bear the thought of his passing. Heroic in his pride and strength, magnificent in his self-possession, he is the father of the anthropoids. It seems incredible that nature can combine in his person such gentleness and such power. Truly it can be said of him 'to know him is to love him'. In captivity he conjures admiration from his keepers with the same felicity that he inspires wonder in the rain-forest. One has only to read *The Year of the Gorilla* by George Schaller and Dian Fossey's more recent studies to realise how proximity breeds respect. Such is the impact of a great male gorilla on the public at large that many have become world-known. In Milwaukee more citizens know of Samson the Gorilla than can name the governor of Wisconsin, or the mayor of the city, and in a study done at the Milwaukee County Zoo, fourteen per cent of the visitors went just to see Samson. Guy, at the London Zoo, is by far its most famous personality and has been dominating audiences for twenty-five years. He was the first gorilla I ever saw, and twenty years ago I visited him regularly and plied him with a tribute of exotic fruits. Stefi of Basle, the founding father of a large band, Snowflake of Barcelona, the only white ape in the world, Sinbad of Lincoln Park, Chicago, a worthy successor to the renowned Bushman who lived to the age of twenty-one, these and many others have gathered much fame. The best-known gorillas of the past included Gargantua of the Ringling circus, Bobby the Giant of Berlin (who weighed over 600 pounds) and Bamboo of Philadelphia.

Perhaps one of the secrets of the gorilla's magnetic appeal is his aloofness. Unlike a chimpanzee, who seems willing to concede man's superiority, at least to the extent of imitating him in his presence, the larger ape retains his reserve. I endorse Sir Julian Huxley's dictum that 'no man can feel anything but humble in the presence of an adult male gorilla'. This conscious feeling of distance not unmixed with disdain is characteristic of gorilla posture and expression. They do not invite familiarity, and resent, as often as not, any unseemly show of affection on the part of a human. The emotional tempo of gorillas is subdued. More than any other ape, including man, they appear to reside in an inner world of self-containment – a carefully guarded proprium of which they alone hold the key.

What little is known about wild gorillas is due largely to Schaller and Fossey who studied the mountain race only. George Schaller writes in *The Mountain Gorilla*

> Probably no animal has fired the imagination of man to the same extent as has the gorilla. Its manlike appearance and tremendous strength, its remote habitat and reputed belligerence, have endowed the beast with a peculiar fascination and stirred popular and scientific interest. It appears to possess some transcendent quality which inspires every visitor to its realm.

Schaller goes on to describe a first encounter with an adult male, or silverback, as they are called because their backs become silvery-grey when they reach maturity. 'He lay on the slope, propped on his huge shaggy arms, and the muscles of his broad shoulders and silver back rippled. He gave an impression of dignity and restrained power, of absolute certainty in his majestic appearance.' I suppose that in the rain-forest the gorilla is master, though no doubt he gives way to the elephant and man. Before the advent of firearms some two hundred years ago he held his own with man. Some believe that he lived in a state of symbiosis with the indigenous human population as a beneficiary of their slash-and-burn agriculture. Raiding the plantations is an immemorial gorilla pastime, and man has provided him with many a meal of manioc, banana, cacao, macabo, maize, sorghum and cola; he in turn being trapped and hunted for protein and harassed by forest destruction. Now the balance has turned crucially against him. Modern firearms, deforestation and the influx of cattle, signal his doom and it is doubtful if he will survive the century in the wild state. The governments of the African states – the Cameroons, Gabon, Zaïre, the Central African Republic – which still harbour gorilla remnants, scarcely understand, or are indeed aware of, the problems. To them the gorilla is a relic of a past of which they feel ashamed. Lip-service they may pay to him, but protect him they will not. The forest that is his ancestral heart-land, and of which he is the highest expression, is being scalped for cash.

When I was in the Kribi area of the Cameroons a few years ago, in what was supposed to be stronghold gorilla country, the families were often twenty or thirty miles apart and terrified of man. Everywhere the primal forest had been decimated and the local tribesmen had acquired modern weapons. N'gee N'gee, as the hunters called him, was in full retreat. After fourteen days of tracking we caught up with a small group of seven or eight near Eboloua, where the resident tribe had no hunting tradition. We saw the animals for only about a minute. They were feeding on Aframomum seeds and gurgling with contentment. When our presence became known they stole away into the penumbra, after the patriarch had taken on board an infant of about a year old who had given a startled shriek. He allowed the baby to clamber up his forearm and take refuge on his back. As they merged into the bosky shadows the infant looked back at us in alarmed curiosity. The incident made the whole trip worth while and remains one of the most memorable of my life.

I first met the great ape in R. M. Ballantyne's absurd book *The Gorilla Hunters* at the age of about twelve, and later I saw him on the screen in *King Kong*. I can remember even then discounting the stories of his innate ferocity and insatiable libido. For years I collected every available book on gorillas, but they were a disappointing miscellany: mainly the narratives of trophy or specimen-hunters and interspersed, for the most part, with photographs of the cadavers of huge sag-jawed males, hand-hoisted to give them the grisly appearance of life. Even in these dim works the mystic allure of the gorilla came through for me in unmistakable terms – it became my ambition to have gorillas as my friends, to win their confidence and trust. To me the gorilla is the closest thing to an embodiment of Rousseau's dream of the Noble Savage. Power buys respect, but restraint of power buys admiration. In the seventeen years that the gorillas of Howletts have lived together no ape has seriously injured another. Seemingly terrible quarrels take place from time to time and probably serve to act as a tension-release sequence, but the fact remains that in spite of the noise and the screaming no permanent damage has ever been recorded. I myself after all this time have never been badly hurt in spite of the fact that few weekends pass without my entering their enclosure and spending an hour or two in their company. The band now numbers sixteen, eight males and eight females, named overleaf in hierarchical order.

THE HOWLETTS GORILLA BAND

(N.B. BIRTH DATES OF WILD-CAUGHT ANIMALS CAN ONLY BE APPROXIMATE.)

Date of birth	Age arrived at Howletts	Name	Weight
Males			
Dec. 1958	10 months	Gugis	360 lb
Sept. 1973 (arrival)	12	Kisoro	320 lb
June 1965	2	Mumbah	252 lb
June 1968	10 months	Djoum	178 lb
June 1971	11 months	Bitam	80 lb
Aug. 1971	9 months	Toumbi	72 lb
2 April 1975	birth	Kijo	20 lb
6 Oct. 1975	birth	Koundu	14 lb
Females			
July 1958	2	Shamba	250 lb
July 1960	$1\frac{1}{2}$	Mouila	210 lb
Jan. 1961	4 months	Baby Doll	205 lb
Feb. 1962	8 months	Ju Ju	185 lb
May 1969	9 months	Mushie	105 lb
April 1971	12 months	Founa	76 lb
30 April 1975	birth	Kimba	19 lb
Jan. 1976 (arrival)	$3\frac{1}{2}$	Sidonie	60 lb

Five of the gorillas in the gorillarium, with some of their exercise and play equipment. Left to right: *Baby Doll, Ju Ju, Founa, Mouila, Bitam*

For many years we used to exercise the gorilla family in the open parkland, but we had to abandon the procedure when Gugis and Shamba reached the ages of nine and ten respectively. We found that the apes were more and more reluctant to return to their enclosures as their confidence increased. For some time we counteracted this tendency by taking them out in the evening and arriving back as darkness fell. Gorillas, like most big primates, are strictly diurnal and like to turn in at sundown. But even this ruse did not work for ever and in September 1967 the Howletts gorilla band had its last ramble. The park only comprises fifty acres and if more land had been available it would have been possible to continue the walks for several more years. By some strange intuition the gorillas knew the boundary and seldom broke it except in late autumn when my neighbour's apples were red and ripe. These they found irresistible, and always looked truant and guilty when they clambered over the fence and stole them.

Even when half grown, the apes would scatter other animals before them, even bison and wild horses. This behaviour has been noted in the wild, when they have been seen to drive red buffalo from a glade where they wished to forage undisturbed.

I have always fostered an ambition to be able to 'go in' with an adult male gorilla. To my knowledge this has only been done once in a zoo, at Basle, where the gifted keeper, Stemmler, used to enter Stefi's enclosure. Stefi is the breeding male of that famous group and enjoyed Stemmler's company. However, after the age of twelve, Stefi became too rough and Stemmler gave up the practice. This fine male had an exceptionally placid disposition which was proved by an incident related to me by Dr Ernst Lang, the Director of the Basle Zoo. One evening, after the zoo was closed, a young girl employed to clean the service corridor tested the door to Stefi's sleeping quarters and found it open. As the door gave way the 350-pound male grabbed her and the door closed automatically, locking them both in. Stefi was so pleased to have company, particularly female company, that he hugged the terrified girl close to his frame and did not release her until the morning, when help arrived. She was shaken and frightened, but unhurt after what was, and is likely to remain, a unique experience.

I have failed with my male gorilla Gugis – but not for want of trying. Until he was eleven years old I played and cuddled with him each weekend, but gradually he began to view me as a rival as well as friend and protector. I was quite happy to concede to him first place in the hierarchy, and on occasion assumed the submission posture to convince him of my good intentions.

Alas! it was all to no avail. In a certain mood he would charge me and release a parabolic swing at my shoulder or plant a punitive bite on some part of my anatomy. In a state of nature, and if I were a gorilla, we would have wrestled together until supremacy had been clearly established. The next male in the pipeline – Mumbah – is already becoming boisterous at the age of eleven and I anticipate that two more years are all we have left together. My hopes rest on the fact that gorillas vary as much as humans in disposition and character, and perhaps in Djoum, Bitam or Toumbi the combination of adulthood and gentleness may emerge.

Females have never presented a problem. All remain reliable. Possibly this is because they can never aspire to the leadership of a band and so never challenge for primacy. As Gugis grew bigger and more aggressive, Shamba and Mouila would act as my bodyguards, seldom leaving my side. An ill-intentioned approach by Gugis would elicit from them a cacophony of barks and screams.

The domination system of training simply does not work with male apes and invites disaster when the animals reach maturity. In Japan a few years ago there was a famous act with three gorillas which had been trained to 'perform' since childhood. The act ended abruptly when the trainer was nearly killed. Circuses often castrate male chimps to render them tractable, a practice which should be outlawed forthwith – as indeed should all acts involving wild animals in circuses.

In the wild state gorillas live in bands or extended families numbering perhaps from ten to thirty, and so it was imperative to create conditions where a large group could run together. All the original apes at Howletts (except the recently-arrived breeding male, Kisoro) were obtained as infants, and each new arrival had to be carefully assimilated into the group structure. At the time of writing we can run fourteen of the sixteen apes together in the big enclosure 100 feet by 60 feet by 30 feet. To see them 'en famille' and to watch their inter-action is a joy which never palls. I know of no other zoo where so many gorillas of different ages and sex can mix freely together. In a month or two we plan to let Kisoro join the band so that for the first time he can take his rightful place as paterfamilias. He has already patted his son Kijo through the bars, tapping him gently on his back with his great padded hands, chortling his affection. We have provided them with eighty ropes, brachiating bars or hand walks, a thirty-foot chute, a heated swimming-pool, an artificial tree in which they can make nests or take shelter from rain or sun, a massive drum, tubular steel spheres, cable reels and truck-tyres. The eternal struggle is against boredom and to encourage play we spread a hundred bales of wheat straw twice a year

in the enclosure, thus providing a comfortable surface for wrestling, climbing, leaping and rolling. Each morning, whatever the weather, we scatter nuts or raisins in this deep litter, which enables the apes to forage for an hour or two, after the manner of wild-living gorillas. At sundown we distribute fresh bales of clean straw to enable them to make their night nests. In our experience females take this labour more seriously than the males, sometimes spending twenty minutes or so perfecting a structure to their satisfaction. Ideally gorillas should be fed intermittently every half-hour or so, but this presents insuperable problems in a colony attended by only two keepers. Wild gorillas will forage for several hours in the morning and evening, resting during the heat of the day. At Howletts they adopt the same routine during the summer months, but remain indoors for lengthy periods in the winter. Only ten or eleven times in an average year in England will the apes refuse to face the weather at all. They particularly resent cold, driving rain and high winds, and are most active in still, humid weather. In the height of the summer we let them sleep out at night if they so wish and sometimes they have remained active until the early hours, beating their chests, hooting and displaying. Schaller and Fossey do not record any midnight corybantics – but this is probably because they themselves were asleep on these occasions.

The subtleties of hierarchical structures are more easily observed in captivity than in the wild state, and possibly the extra tensions that are built up and exaggerated by confinement tend to expose them with a greater clarity. The dominant role of the male is indicated at a very early age by his overt concern for the safety of his companions. Upon his massive back will fall the burden of group defence; thus Djoum, even at the age of two, responded to outside threats which left Mushie unconcerned. The adult gorilla male who succeeds to the patriarchate of a band is usually a stable and benevolent leader, but not necessarily the largest or most powerful. He is the one who carries the confidence of the females and young black-backs. He must be a skilled botanist and topographer, and from him the whole group will draw its tone and personality. Gorillas have developed an extraordinary capacity to neutralise any overweening intra-familial exercise of power. A juvenile that is attacked by a large male or female is immediately helped by others in the clan – whatever the cause of the assault. The patriarch can usually stifle a quarrel by a series of staccato grunts or coughs – provided that he is near enough. This tendency to go to the assistance of the weaker or outnumbered acts as a counterbalance and enables the extended family to survive without injury. Fights to the death are almost unknown, and often two bands will meet and intermingle without

(above) *A gorilla ramble* (below) *The gorillarium*   25

incident. The gorilla, unlike the chimpanzee, has a high emotional threshold. He is not easily excited. Chimpanzees will welcome me into their enclosure with obvious joy – not so the gorilla. The thongs of affection that bind the gorilla are hidden in his fur. Sometimes an hour will pass before all the gorillas have paid me their respects on entering their enclosure. The gorilla is aloof and distant, and although he uses as many vocalisations as a chimpanzee he is covert in their expression.

Vernon Reynolds believes that chimpanzees are noisy because they are essentially frugivores. When a chimpanzee finds a tree that has plenty of ripe and edible fruit, it gives forth a series of clarion calls and hoots that can be heard for two or three miles, so informing every clansman in hearing of the good news. His cousin, the gorilla, is mainly a pith, leaf and root eater and has no difficulty in locating his diet. Up to two hundred species of plant have been identified as gorilla feed, and in fact the larger ape enjoys the primal role of ground-based herbivore. At Howletts we supply the apes with over ninety types of food a year.

FOOD CONSUMED PER ANNUM BY HOWLETTS GORILLA BAND

Regular Items		*Seasonal Items*	
5,000 lb	Apples	1,000 lb	Sweet corn (whole plant)
5,000 lb	Hawthorn/Ilex	500 lb	Kale
	Maple/Sycamore leaves	500 lb	Leeks
5,000 pints	Milk	500 lb	Peaches
3,000 lb	Bananas	400 lb	Radishes
3,000 lb	Celery	300 lb	Capsicum
3,000 lb	Lettuce	250 lb	Chicory
2,500 bottles	Ribena	250 lb	Plums
1,500 lb	Cucumbers/	200 lb	Fennel
	Tomatoes	200 lb	Mangoes
1,500 lb	Oranges	200 lb	Okra
1,000 lb	Grapes	200 lb	Sugar Cane
1,000 lb	Mazuri Primate Diet	200 lb	Sweet Potatoes
	(Primate Nuts with	150 lb	Broad Beans
	trace elements and	150 lb	Convolvulus
	vitamins)	150 lb	Peas

Regular items (cont.)		Seasonal items (cont.)	
1,000 lb	Pears	100 lb	Brazil Nuts
750 lb	Cabbage	100 lb	Chestnuts
750 lb	Grapefruit	100 lb	Hazelnuts
750 lb	Meat	100 lb	Marrow
500 lb	Dates/Peaches/ Prunes/Sultanas	100 lb	Runner Beans
		100 lb	Walnuts
500 lb	Onions	50 lb	Cherries
500 lb	Parsnips	50 lb	Grass Roots
500 lb	Pineapples	300 lb	Beech/Sweet Chestnut/ Oak leaves and twigs
500 lb	Potatoes		
500 lb	Watercress	30 lb	Blackcurrants
300 lb	Peanuts	30 lb	Celeriac
250 lb	Lemons	30 lb	Parsley
250 lb	Turnips	30 lb	Rose leaves and stems
200 dozen	Eggs	30 lb	Salsify
100 lb	Wheat	30 lb	Sea Kale
60 lb	Chocolate	30 lb	Sorrel
40 lb	Rice	25 lb	Raspberries
30 lb	Barley	25 lb	Strawberries
25 lb	Salt	20 lb	Asparagus
20 lb	Honey	20 lb	Mint
20 lb	Treacle	10 lb	Basil
5 lb	Juniper Berries	10 lb	Blackberries
20 gallons	Beer	10 lb	Chinese Gooseberries
		10 lb	Dill
		10 lb	Figs/ Dried Figs/Dried Apricots/Currants
		10 lb	Tarragon

Occasional Items

200 lb	Brown Bread	20 lb	Jams
100 lb	Lychees	10 lb	Guava
100 lb	Pomegranates	5 lb	Dry Ginger Roots
40 lb	Uglis	5 lb	Horlicks
20 lb	Cocoa	30 lb	Custard Apples

We feel this is important, for in captivity variety is literally the spice of life for a fastidious ape. Wild gorillas get animal protein from the micro-organisms present in large quantities on tropical vegetation, but in temperate climates protein additives are necessary. We feed each animal about one kilo of meat per week, usually roasted or in the form of a stew. Food is a prominent cultural dimension in a wild-living primate and this dimension can to some extent be retained in captivity. It has always shocked me to see the limited fare of many zoo gorillas. The provision of bulk, vitamins and trace elements is not enough except in theory as a gorilla band like a human army marches on its stomach. Wild gorillas tend to carry huge paunches which would horrify many zoo directors who are concerned with overweight and lack of exercise.

Gorillas, like other apes, have a curious capacity to retain physical fitness in zoos even when kept in cramped conditions. Their musculature never seems to lose its tone. No one has to my knowledge fully understood the process whereby they can mobilise muscle so effectively. Pound for pound the gorilla is far stronger than any man, and a full-grown male of average size (350 pounds) could easily handle five heavyweight boxers – muzzled. The gorilla has extraordinary power in his hand grip. This is connected with his ability to walk on his knuckles. He has massive weight-bearing wrists and padded hands which form a terrible weapon of defence. A gorilla in the wild has been said to tear off a man's calf with a wrench of his hand. I advise any reader who remains in doubt as to the power and scope of this ape to go to the Milwaukee Zoo and gaze at Samson – the most impressive primate I have ever seen. Sam La Malfa, his keeper, regards him with awe and with affection and, in his own words, Samson is a 'good boy', reliable and restrained. It is in the restraint of his awesome powers that the gorilla finds his nobility. In the remarkable film *Gorilla* featuring the game warden Adrian De Schruyver and his experience with a mountain gorilla band in Eastern Zaïre, one is amazed at the gentleness of the leading male. Though on several occasions angry enough with De Schruyver to threaten him, he always pulled back from giving the lethal blow.

On one occasion the big male Gugis escaped, and in the process released five other adults into the service passage, which was only four feet wide. The resident veterinary surgeon of the time, Mr Andrew, had made a grave error which was to cost him dearly. I was in the process of giving the gorillas some empty sacks to play with, and asked Andrew to hand a few through to Gugis and the other adults inside the sleeping quarters. He must have had a mental aberration, for he opened the heavy barred door to fling in the sacks. Gugis, hearing the clinking of the key followed by the clanking of the sliding door, rushed

Gugis. The slightly withdrawn lips are a sign of annoyance

inside to see what was afoot. He sized up the situation in a second, shoved the terrified veterinary surgeon aside, bit him severely in the arm and escaped into the passage followed by Shamba, Mouila, Baby Doll and Ju Ju. I heard the frightful screams of Andrew, who no doubt thought his last moment had come, and rushed to the scene of the commotion. I entered the corridor and shouted at Gugis in stentorian tones, ordering him back into his cage. In the crisis, I instinctively tried to reassert my old parental authority. To my astonishment, Gugis, followed by several females, obligingly re-entered his den. The veterinary surgeon was moaning in the kitchen and *hors de combat*. My problem was that as I pulled the sliding doors together I could not find the padlock to fasten them. By the time I had located it several yards away, out of my immediate reach, Gugis had reassessed the situation. I saw his scheming eyes look at the padlock and then at me. With a sudden movement he wrenched open the door I was attempting to hold fast and shouldered me aside contemptuously. My bluff was truly called, but I am glad to say not punished. A few minutes later the animals were charging around the garden harvesting the raspberries, strawberries and blackcurrants and smashing their way through the greenhouse. I summoned all available help and, with the aid of live chickens held upside down, squawking and fluttering, we drove all the apes back into their enclosures with the exception of Baby Doll, who was loose for hours. Eventually the fear of darkness and the lure of a whole bottle of green chartreuse, a delicacy which she had previously experienced only in the smallest doses, were enough to enable her to decide that her old home was the best place to return to, after all. The following morning she held her head in her hands and groaned sadly. We administered Fernet Branca and Alka-Seltzer to good effect.

The three large male gorillas and Bustah, the dominant chimpanzee, get a pint of beer three times a week. The beer round is restricted to these four from motives of economy qualified by a full understanding of male privilege. As in all social primates including man, male dominance is the natural order of things. This point is emphasised by marked sexual dimorphism. The adult male is twice the size of the average female. This factor is common to all the higher primates in varying degrees. It is the supreme arrogance to suppose that this development, itself the work of countless millennia, is a waste of time. Women's liberation makes little sense in the world of primates. Matters simply were not decided that way, and to deny this is to fly in the face of aeons of evolutionary field experiment. In the decision-making, in the actuality of leadership, in defence and in peace-keeping within the band, the male is dominant and can be seen to be dominant. The role of the female is of course just as necessary, just as important, but to elevate it beyond its natural range is to invite disaster.

It seems from the wild studies that a gorilla patriarch is usually of a tolerant, even benevolent, disposition, but this is not always the case in captivity. Possibly the frustration of confinement with its reduced behavioural repertoire erodes some of the apes' essential good nature. Mood watching and mood interpretation are the secrets of survival if one is to retain any tactile relationship with a four-hundred-pound adult gorilla. One mistake can be expensive. Recently my daughter Jamunda misread the signs when feeding some Marmite sandwiches to Gugis, an animal she has known since birth. She paid for her error with eighteen stitches in her hand.

The sculptor, David Wynne, postulates the theory that fear is the magical ingredient that can ennoble a man's relationship with a wild animal. The love of a man for his pet, for his spaniel or his horse, is of a different genre from the love of a man for a tiger or rhinoceros, untrammelled as the latter must be by any attempt to train or discipline. Fear is probably born of the race memory from that great reach of time when the mammals were our competitors. Nascent in this fear is respect, and from a fusion of them both is distilled a pure love and understanding. A love to find which you risk everything and expect nothing back except the stake. How does one describe it to others – make them understand? Perhaps these curious joys will ever remain the delight of an esoteric few. Perhaps denatured man has lurched too far along the road that leads away from wilderness. Perhaps the man-made crevasse will be the one structure to survive him, and most likely of all, perhaps, by the time he rediscovers himself his kindred will have been butchered at his hand.

I only hope that the great gorilla can call on enough friends to save him from extinction. We have killed him for his protein, hunted him for sport with ·480 rifles that have the stopping-power of several tons, we have slaughtered him for the museums and captured him for exhibition in zoo and circus. Worst of all, we have scalped his forest, purloined his ancestral lands and sent in the cattle to ensure that nothing will ever grow again for him. All his strength and courage; all his cumulative wisdom cannot help him now. He calls out to us, to you and me to render back to him what was once his own. Time alone will tell whether his voice will be heard and heeded.

It is a long and painstaking process to gain the confidence and trust of gorillas, and to get to know and appreciate their separate personalities. The wide range of characterisation is reflected in the varied physiognomies that the apes present to us. Physical differences are probably more noticeable in the Howletts

3. (above) *Gugis* 4. (below) *Dingy, Gugis and Ju Ju*

band than in a wild family as all the twelve original gorillas were wild caught and unlikely to be closely related. (Except for Bitam and Founa, who came from Congo-Brazzaville, and Toumbi who was shipped from Gabon, the others were all born in the Southern Cameroons.) The one advantage of this lack of connection is the wide gene pool that it provides. We should have few problems of inbreeding for several generations to come. Observers of wild gorillas remark on the striking family resemblances displayed by different groups, reinforced as they are by similarities of temperament and disposition. Certainly, from my experience of visiting other gorillas in world zoos, I would say that their individual physical differences are on a par with our own. I will now try and introduce the reader to each gorilla in turn, in order of seniority.

Shamba, the oldest at about nineteen years, is definitely the top female, though she has recently been challenged for.this position by Mouila. She remains, however, firmly in charge whenever the two great males are absent. Shamba's naturally dominant character is reinforced by a massive physique. She is the largest female in the band as well as the oldest. Both these factors are important but not decisive in the struggle for status. When we put twelve of the gorillas together (the whole group except the two adult males Gugis and Kisoro and the hand-reared babies), and I enter the enclosure for an hour's relaxation, Shamba is usually the last to pay her respects. In fact, I often seek her out and settle close to her as a respite from the boisterous overtures of Mumbah and Djoum. Such is her prestige that proximity to her is a guarantee of immunity. I can remember that on the last few occasions that I played with Gugis in person she never left my side, and her presence was comforting as Gugis, then eleven years old and weighing 300 lb, was by that time a most unreliable companion. It was largely thanks to her protection that I came out of these last encounters unscathed.

Shamba is noticeably moodier than the other three adult females and I hesitate to touch or tickle her without an invitation. The head gorilla keeper, Richard Johnstone-Scott, seldom goes in with her, as on one occasion she chased him out of the cage with 'intent to harm'! Whether this range of mood is to some extent a concomitant of her high social position is hard to say. She enjoys playing with the younger trio, Bitam, Founa and Toumbi, and on one occasion I saw her with all three on her broad back.

Shamba is undoubtedly the greediest of the gorillas and can be ill-tempered at feeding time both with her companions and with us. In fact we virtually have to feed her alone in a shut-off to prevent her mopping up several other dinners.

She is an exceptionally handsome specimen with clear-cut features. Compare her face with Baby Doll's and notice the lack of nodulous irregularities. Shamba has, as befits her social position, a commanding expression and a short temper. These, I am glad to say, disguise an affectionate temperament and a warm heart. Once I was alone with her in her sleeping quarters, and inadvisedly handed some of her uneaten fruit through the mesh to Mouila and JuJu, who were next door. She cursed me with a barrage of staccato barks that elicited from me a counter-display of ill temper motivated by fear. After this swearing bout I retired to sit on some straw and sulk. To my amazement and delight she came and embraced me with an overt display of affection which, typically, included a gentle drumming on my back. I answered her gurgles with my own and we both bathed in the joys of rapprochement. Gorillas have expressive eyes and the emotional messages conveyed thereby are strikingly similar to our own. Rage – hatred – fear – love – surprise – disappointment – all are clearly discernible, at least to the practised eye.

Of all the gorillas at Howletts only Gugis surpasses Shamba in classical beauty. His claim to perfection is marred by the smallness and, dare I say it, the meanness of his eyes. Compare them with Kisoro's. Gugis's eyes, alas, are the windows of his soul. The magnificent structure of his personality is faulted by treachery and jealousy. Gugis has been with me since he was one year old, but it was not until his eighth year that traces of his erratic nature appeared for the first time. He had always been a 'mother's boy', seemingly in greater need of affection than his contemporary, Shamba. At the first sign of alarm he would climb into my arms or on to my back for safety. Always the possessor of magnetic charm, he was the constant recipient of love in abundance from his surrogate mother, Mrs Dorothy Hastings. (The mother of my first wife, Jane. She hand-reared Kivu – who died after nine months – Shamba, Gugis, Baby Doll.) I was drawn to him partly because of his special personality and partly because he was the first male that we had reared. The first intimation of trouble came when we were rambling in the park in the summer of 1966. Gugis embraced me with a friendly grunt and then settled in my lap as I propped myself against the bole of a large chestnut tree. I returned his gesture with a kiss on his neck, but was rewarded with a bite on the cheek. Gugis ran off immediately and I was annoyed enough to chase him for over a hundred yards – my *amour propre* in worse shape than my face, which was merely grazed. I disregarded the incident, giving my favourite ape the benefit of any doubt as to his real intentions: I could not willingly believe that resentment lurked in the recesses of his psyche. However a few months later he put on a repeat per-

Shamba sitting on the cable reel

formance – this time in his sleeping quarters. Once again he bit me in the face whilst appearing to solicit affection.

As the years unfolded it became apparent that Gugis had a flaw in his character that would make it impossible for me to go in with him when full grown. This strange aberration could be described as emotional treachery, purporting to be in one mood when actually in another. At best he seemed to suffer from exceptional volatility of mood, unsignalled at that. These failings were eventually common knowledge among the other gorillas, and in the wild state it is doubtful if Gugis could ever have aspired to the patriarchate of a family. The females, though fond of him, are uneasy in his presence as they are likely to be the unwilling recipients of his redirected aggression. They seldom play when he is with them as play requires relaxation. Whether this distrust of him impairs his ability to breed successfully I do not know. Over the last six years Gugis has been observed copulating with Shamba, Mouila and JuJu many times, but with Baby Doll only once. We decided that if we bred successfully from Kisoro, we would tranquilise Gugis and find out whether he is impotent or infertile. Johnstone-Scott has noticed that he tends to take it out of the females after copulation and questions whether this impatience is due to a failure to climax. We have found it impossible to put him with the five youngest members of the colony. He simply has no patience with infants, and seems to resent the attention lavished on them by the keepers and adult females. We have steeled our nerves several times and opened the shutter separating him from the young gorillas, but always with depressing results. On the last occasion he picked up Mushie and flung her fifteen feet in the air. Fortunately she landed on the deep litter unhurt. Many zoos have experienced similar behaviour with their silver-back males but quite a number settle down and become good fathers. In the wild state this problem is unknown, considerable intra-familial tolerance being the order of things.

To give Gugis his due, his bark can be worse than his bite. I once opened the wrong hatch in error and watched him charge in among the young ones. To my horror he rushed up to Djoum, then only three years old. Djoum jumped on to Mouila's shoulders for protection but no sooner there than Gugis's mouth closed on his back. Later, when we examined Djoum in trepidation, we could not find a mark. We know that he enjoys 'teasing', but to us his actions betray an uncertain temper. Of course it is expected of all adult males to show aggression from time to time, but with the average animal this mood is clearly signalled by a withdrawal of the lips, erection of body hair and side-glancing stares. The eyes, in fact, as in a human, express most clearly oncoming emotional

Gugis displaying

storms fuelled by jealousy, anger or even fear.

It is easier to believe some of the exploits of the Norse berserks as passed down in the Icelandic sagas after one has witnessed the inordinate strength of an ape possessed. A classic example is the exploit of Thorolf Skallagrimsson at the battle of Brunanburgh in A.D. 937.

> Thorolf became so furious [i.e. berserk] that he threw his shield on his back, and, taking the spear with both hands, rushed forwards striking and thrusting on both sides. Men turned away from him, but he killed many. Thus he cleared his way to the standard of Hring [one of the enemy leaders], and nothing could stand against him. He killed the men who bore it, and cut down the standard pole. Then he thrust the spear into the breast of the jarl through his coat of mail and his body, so that it came out between his shoulders; he raised him on the spear over his head, and put the shaft down into the ground. The jarl expired on the spear, in sight of foes and friends.

An American primate research centre has recorded a pull of 1,350 pounds from a female chimpanzee weighing only 120 pounds. These seizures are of rare occurrence and, preceded as they are by an elaborate display sequence, serve no doubt to deter any would-be aggressors or rivals. Gorillas, like most simians, are capable of group response to a sudden threat. This reaction can be stimulated by a certain high-intensity shriek of alarm. On one occasion I remember taking a London newspaper photographer for a gorilla walk, after warning him that some of the apes might wish to climb on him and examine his person out of curiosity. I advised him, in this event, to remain calm and wait until the inspection was completed, and on no account attempt to free himself by force. The inevitable happened of course. JuJu clambered up the stranger, who soon panicked and tried to disengage himself. JuJu screamed in fear, thinking that she was under attack, and an instant later six gorillas were heading for the fray. If I had not managed to extricate JuJu from his arms instantly he would have been badly mauled. As it was he showed no inclination to continue the walk, his camera having anyway suffered mortal damage in the scuffle.

Gugis uses a wide range of vocalisations and signs to indicate his needs. He has, for instance, several different ways of signifying hunger. The mildest is a good-natured rumbling grunt roughly the equivalent of 'yum-yum'. A chorus of such sounds anticipates the arrival of the evening meal or the dispersal of a sack of nuts or currants. In JuJu this utterance is sometimes extended to a high-pitched chant of anticipation. At the next level of demand Gugis blows through his lips and achieves an effect that could be described as oral flatulence. The message here is specific – he is requesting a food item that is at hand and is in view. More emphatic still is a loud kissing sound, and if this fails he has one further ploy, stuffing straw through the bars or mesh of his cage in a final effort to gain attention. As a last resort this is usually successful, for if no food is forthcoming he persists until there is an unpleasant mess to clear up. To some extent gorillas can understand language, particularly when it concerns them directly. If I say to my wife 'I think I will go and fetch some beer for the gorillas', Gugis will quietly go to the aperture where I hand him his can of light ale. Only the three big males, Gugis, Kisoro and Mumbah, get beer, usually about twice a week. Mumbah, being the youngest, shakes the can in order to make it squirt when he pulls out the ring cap, but Gugis never wastes a drop, being far too old for such frivolities. Kisoro, a recent arrival, has not yet mastered the technique of can-opening and holes the tin with his canine, laboriously sucking out each drop to the protracted envy of his attendant females. The empty cans then become playthings for the juveniles, who incorporate them in their various games, such as 'tag', 'catch-as-catch-can', 'round and round the mulberry bush' and 'I'm the king of the castle'.

Mouila is in appearance and character what a young adult gorilla female of sixteen years is expected to be – indeed a model ape. At 200 pounds she is neither too fat nor too thin. Second only to Shamba in status, she lives out a comparatively stress-free existence. This happy state is evident from her perfectly groomed appearance. Broadly speaking, plucking out body hair is confined in captivity to low-ranking adults; a finding that is reflected in Jane Goodall's study of wild-living chimpanzees in the Gombi forest, *In the Shadow of Man*. Molly Badham, who has had great success in breeding primates at Twycross Zoo near Atherstone, believes that 'plucking' is contagious and advises strongly against introducing a confirmed plucker into a vice-free colony. Of recent years Baby Doll and JuJu, the worst offenders on this score in the past, have almost abandoned this habit, which remains prevalent however among our chimpanzee family. In fact the chimps have added a refinement – social plucking – which appears to be a weird exaggeration of their deep-seated impulse to groom each other.

Mouila is tolerant of the young gorillas and will spend an hour or so each day playing with them good-naturedly. She shows a slight preference for Founa, whereas Shamba leans to the company of Bitam. It is interesting to note here that even at the weight of 252 pounds the young male Mumbah has not developed enough confidence to challenge any of the senior females. Even

40

Mouila giving me a love-bite

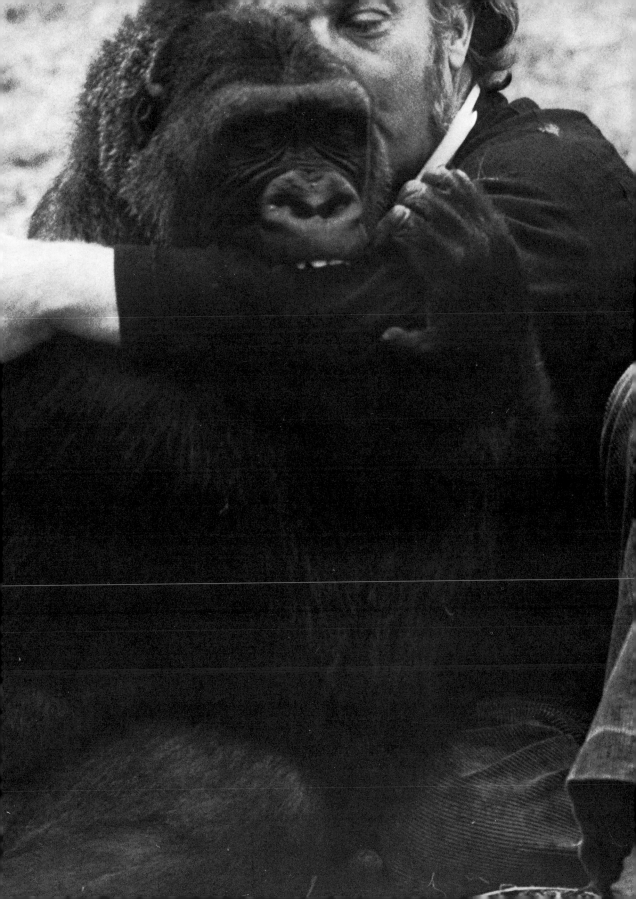

Ju Ju at 185 pounds has preserved some of her ascendancy over the eleven-year-old black-back. This status quo cannot last much longer as, at this stage of growth, Mumbah puts on one pound of weight a week – soon sheer size will settle the issue. George Schaller noted that all adult males rank above all females in the wild state. I know of one case in a private zoo – Gordon Mills's colony of gorillas at Weybridge, Surrey – where the resident male Olly is completely dominated by a combination of two large females to the extent that no copulation has ever been observed. Olly is however an unusually small male. The dominance factor is a crucial one in the breeding of apes, though not perhaps to the degree required for the elephant tribe. Dr John F. Eisenberg's study of the Ceylon elephant confirms that a cow will only accept a bull's advances when paralysed by fear of him. With apes and man the situation is less drastic, but clear-cut – to present to a male is to submit to him and the process incorporates an ingredient of fear. The presentation posture is also used by gorillas of both sexes as an asexual gesture of submission. If such an abject genuflection is undertaken but not honoured, this causes strident resentment from the sufferers. I have several times seen Gugis break the rules of sanctuary by delivering an unpleasant bite on the offered back. Such treachery invites the wrath of hell from the rest of the band, and a rapid getaway is usually prearranged.

Whereas a human offers the weapon-empty hand for a mutual shake, the gorilla offers his unprotected arm as hostage – I have seldom seen this gesture abused. The origin of the human kiss can be understood by watching gorillas interact. Gorillas only kiss as a begging gesture for food; food that is in the process of being eaten by a high-ranking ape. The apes have a useful regurgitating mechanism which provides them with a 'dessert' of half-digested food. Anthropologists believe that prehistoric woman used this technique to provide her offspring with mouth-to-mouth feeding, thus adumbrating the celebrated kiss. As a means of conveying affection, gorillas embrace in a standing position and gurgle contentedly, sometimes gently drumming with the palm of the hand on each other's backs. A reunion after a long separation will usually elicit this greeting, which is often accompanied by a partial closing of the eyes. Another movement which appears to bond-strengthen the females is the head-to-tail tandem dance. I have often seen Shamba, Mouila and Ju Ju cling to each other in this fashion; for some reason this behaviour is often stimulated by oestrus. In view of the absence of outside threats and family relationships, it is surprising how cohesive and content are the Howletts gorillas. One always has the feeling that behind the indifferent emotional facade, behind the aloofness,

42

an undercurrent of almost passionate unity exists. I can get the gorillas, even Gugis, to rush to my defence if I stage a mock fight with a stranger. This is a crucial test, and a successful response confirms one's status as a valued member of the band.

The odd-girl-out in the colony is Baby Doll, originally named Yaounde. She was dumped in my bed by an animal dealer who had just returned from West Africa, when only sixteen weeks old and weighing 7 lb. Baby Doll is the only gorilla in the group who may have suffered from human imprintation, as she has never managed to integrate completely with the others. She may of course be a genuine eccentric, but the fact of her early capture and the possibilities of psychic disturbances cannot be denied. She ranks lower than she should for an ape of her size and personality, and this could be because she is less able to call on friends in an argument. To compensate for this, however, she has become adept at handling Gugis and Kisoro, and takes greater liberties with the two great silverbacks than any other female. She is the only gorilla who plays with Gugis with any appearance of enjoyment, and in return he treats her with an easy tolerance seldom extended to the others. Baby Doll has little fear of strange phenomena, and even squeaky toys and rubber snakes that inspire terror in Shamba and Mouila leave her unmoved except by curiosity. When in possession of such an object she relishes the advantage it confers. Placing it on her head or tucking it between her legs she wanders where she wills – the other gorillas giving her a wide berth. Baby Doll has always been the tomboy of the family, with a preference for the rough horse-play beloved of the young males. Hair-pulling, sweater-grabbing, back-thumping and, worst of all, jump-crushing are all part of her repertoire. The last-named pursuit is not very enjoyable for the human participant, as it entails jumping down from up to twelve feet above and smashing you to the ground. All in the best of fun, but quite dangerous if one is not prepared or if one is inside the sleeping quarters without the protection of the foot-thick carpet of wheat straw.

Baby Doll is the only adult who shows any paedomorphic traits. She is a thumb-sucker and a window-gazer. These habits have persisted down to the present time. The first is a classic displacement activity well known to psycho-analysts, the latter a left-over from her hand-reared infancy. The cottage where she lived until her third year is in full view of the gorilla complex, and she will brave rain and wind on some evenings to gaze longingly at the lights and listen to the sounds of voices and merriment in which she can no longer take her part. On these occasions my daughter and I will slip out and feed her morsels from our own fare, which may serve to lessen her misery and sense of loss.

Richard Johnstone-Scott has a special attachment to Baby Doll and I would hazard a guess that she runs a close second to his wife in the race for his affections.

Kisoro mates with her each oestrus, sometimes lifting his leg in an angular fashion seemingly to get better penetration. Baby Doll missed out three monthly periods at the end of 1974 and we had high hopes for her. However a urine test proved negative and she 'came in' again. We feel she may have aborted internally and reabsorbed the foetus, not an unusual occurrence among primates during first pregnancies. Now she has given birth, and the day was one of rejoicing at Howletts – a day almost of atonement, as we feel in her case a measure of guilt for the degree of her isolation.

An extraordinary event took place in the gorillarium one weekend in early 1975. Gugis smashed through the heavy iron bars of the shut-off where he sleeps alone at night, and entered Shamba's sleeping quarters. She, being five months pregnant, was also alone. Gugis beat her up in spite of the fact that she dashed outside into the open-air run to escape from him. The enormous strength Gugis must have deployed in tearing his way through the bars was obvious from the damage. Shamba had to spend several hours in the cold on a wet February morning until help arrived at 8.30 a.m. We believe Gugis made his break-through at about three or four in the morning. Shamba's massive frame and figure stood her in good stead, also no doubt her ancient bond with Gugis, who in the event only administered a magisterial thrashing. Long ago we accepted the fact that Gugis would take it out of a lone female, and always made a point of putting never less than two of them in with him at the same time. The only female that he does not treat in this cavalier manner is Baby Doll. Could this forbearance be due to a lack of sexual interest? Ernst Lang told me that at Basle he had noticed that Stefi, the resident male, would often beat up a female and then copulate with her. After this piece of information from so successful a breeder we left Mouila with Gugis for a whole night, and in the morning we found her in a sorry state. We never dared take the risk again.

The two keepers and I have noticed that the arrival of Kisoro in September 1973 has unsettled Gugis to a marked degree. In the pre-Kisoro era his bad moods were infrequent but now they seem to predominate. The tension that is within him finds expression in teeth-grinding and straw-eating. The biblical 'gnashing' and compulsive eating are both familiar stress-release activities among humans.

One advantage derived from Kisoro's inclusion in the group is the deflection

of Baby Doll's calf-love from Richard to himself. In the old days Baby Doll, gaining scant satisfaction from Gugis during the four or five days of her oestrus, would 'present' to Richard without success. Before Kisoro's arrival he had only observed Gugis mating with her on one occasion. Baby Doll's passion for her keeper had become an awkward fixation, and receiving no satisfaction whatsoever she sometimes retaliated with open aggression. To the welcome relief of them both, Kisoro mates with her consistently at the appropriate times.

Baby Doll, though a trifle knock-elbowed, is a fine physical specimen. She carries less belly than the others and her crumpled face is capable of a wide range of expression. Baby Doll has mystery – a strange allure – a capacity to elicit interest that separates her in some subtle way from the other apes. Is this special quality derived from her humanised babyhood? I think not, or at least not entirely. Her quaintness and eccentricity is part and parcel of her endowment. Uncompetitive and unconscious of rank, she has her own brand of courage. In unfamiliar surroundings she retains her self-possession. On the four or five occasions that the adults have escaped *en masse*, only Baby Doll has had the presence of mind to fully capitalise on her freedom – and each time Baby Doll was the last to be driven, cajoled or decoyed back into the enclosure. As Richard has discovered, the best way of getting her to do something is by pretending to want her to do the opposite. In the course of time she has even rumbled this stratagem. Bluff, double bluff and counter-bluff, she is aware of every move in the game. When closeted with a higher-ranking female like Mouila, she modifies her behaviour to enable me to feed her without arousing the senior ape's attention. I will hide a tit-bit in my clothing and slip it to her when Mouila's interest is engaged elsewhere. When this has been accomplished she will devour the food soundlessly. By the time that Mouila is aware that anything is up nothing remains but an innocent look on the face of the plotters. Baby Doll, apart from Gugis, is the only ape to 'blow raspberries' when soliciting food, but she only makes this noise when alone or in the company of junior animals. A mode of behaviour common to gorillas is balancing various objects on their heads: Baby Doll indulges in this habit more often than the others. This activity has frequently been observed in the wild and its significance is obscure. (Gorillas also use their thigh-pits to carry things in the manner that a human will put an object under his arm.) Baby Doll is something of a recluse, and her behaviour suggests that, if given the opportunity, she would wish from time to time to get completely away from the whole band. In the wild state some gorillas are known to go off on their own

46

for days at a time, but observation tells us that this habit is usually confined to adult males, some of whom, it is believed, become virtual solitaries.

Slightly younger than Baby Doll and smaller in stature is the redoubtable JuJu. In the February of 1974 she, along with Kisoro and Mouila, contracted a virus infection which drove her to the edge of death. The other two apes recovered after a mild set-back, but JuJu wasted away until she was merely a living skeleton. The virus was unidentified and at one point we all despaired of her life. We spent the nights by her side, and though our presence brought comfort, in typical gorilla fashion she showed little overt sign of appreciation. Nevertheless the all-night vigils paid off, as we continually plied her with soups and gruels to prevent a fatal dehydration. Gorillas tend to blame the nearest available person or ape for their plight, I suppose with some logic, but in some way they seem to understand the depth of feeling that motivates their human friends. JuJu, thanks to the skills of the resident vet., Tom Begg, and most important of all, thanks to her own indomitable will, managed to haul her way through to survival. Her convalescence lasted a full two months, but by August 1974, she was pregnant to Kisoro – an extraordinary turnabout of fortune.

Bassa with Ju Ju, then pregnant to Kisoro

JuJu, though basically an orthodox gorilla, has one or two habits peculiar to her alone. One of these is a mild form of flagellation. She enjoys being gently whipped by a slender wand about the head or arms. She will sometimes approach me with a suitable cane of her own selection and press it into my hand. Having done this she will adopt a cowering posture and await, with delight, a rain of blows, provided they are not administered with too great severity. A gorilla flagellant must be something of a rarity, even on a world scale. JuJu is the gentlest and most reliable of all the adults and we entrusted our son, Bassa, to her embrace when he was only six months old. (See colour plate 6) As he grew older, Bassa learnt to ride on her back and, even at a late stage of pregnancy, she delighted at his appearance and cried at his departure. The only danger inherent in the Ju Ju–Bassa relationship was due to Bassa's inability to 'cling' in quadrumanal fashion like a true Pongoid. In the event of JuJu climbing to the roof of the thirty-foot-high cage with Bassa in her arms, a fall would be probable. Ju Ju, much to our relief, seemed aware of Bassa's deficiency in this respect and never attempted to leave the ground. If one had to pick an animal as a foster-mother to a human baby I would unhesitatingly choose the terrestrial gorilla in preference to any other ape. I have known of two occasions when gorillas have 'adopted' other species. The most famous example of this was the love of Mrs Hoyt's huge female gorilla, Toto, for a cat. Toto remained faithful to her 'pet' until it died, whereupon, after a decent pause, she chose another from a litter of six kittens. Toto treated her charges with the utmost care and affection, and a similar experience has been recorded at the impresario Gordon Mills's Weybridge colony. Here, Olly, before the arrival of his two companions, was presented with a young puppy as a playmate. Olly took to it immediately and the two became inseparable. So attached to the puppy did Olly become that his owner decided to end the experiment for fear of imprintation.

Gorillas, unlike chimps, seldom show hostility to small mammals, though they have a built-in fear of snakes. Chimps, being partial carnivores, will soon kill and eat any small animal or bird that comes their way, and in the wild will even take part in organised hunts. Not so the gorilla; in the presence of a strange furry animal he is moved by mild curiosity, tempered by alarm if the creature is outside the range of his experience. Once a rabbit sneaked into the ape compound, and when the gorillas began to play in the morning they flushed it from a pile of straw. For a moment they stood back astonished. Chimps or primitive man would have killed it without delay and without difficulty as the deep litter impeded its movement. The gorillas responded according to temperament and role. Gugis, after a timid examination, tried to hide it from view by burying it with straw. Mouila and Shamba nervously ran their finger-pads through its fur and recoiled every time it moved. Baby Doll tried to pick it up and carry it as if it was some kind of animated toy. We managed to extract the rabbit unscathed and free it in the garden. Gorilla race-memory seems to provide them with a fear of snakes and fungi. We once tried them with fresh mushrooms and they showed undisguised repugnance. This tolerance towards small mammals does not extend to the rat. Once or twice in the morning we have found dead but untouched rats on the floor, apparently smashed by a blow on the head. George Schaller describes an incident when he saw a whole band of gorillas by-pass a sitting ground-dove that had had the temerity to build its nest in the middle of a gorilla trail. Only the infants stopped to examine the bird, one of them gently touching its head. The fear of snakes seems universal among primates. Many keepers use a rubber snake to frighten animals from one enclosure to the other or as a protective talisman. We have never been driven to this expedient or for that matter to the use of an electric stick. The latter is a device used in 'working' circus animals.

The next male in the pipeline after Gugis and Kisoro is Mumbah. He is now just eleven years old and touching 252 lb. Though extremely rough in play and a confirmed sweater-grabber, he remains friendly and affectionate to his limited circle of human friends. Sweater-grabbing, which is Mumbah's favourite game, is an expensive one. He has destroyed dozens of my finest cashmeres during the past year. I have tried to wean him from this vice but without success. The most unpleasant experience I had on this account was during a television sequence being shot for the 'Nationwide' programme. I had no desire to be stripped before ten million viewers, so I wore a heavy oiled-wool jumper which I thought was pull-proof. This unfortunately proved to be the case, as at one point, when I was distracted by my own commentary, Mumbah wrenched the garment with such violence that I was knocked out against the metal tree. The material held, and fortunately so did my head, which still bears the scar. The drama was an unexpected bonus for the programme.

Unlike Gugis and Kisoro, Mumbah is tolerant of small gorillas and only asserts his authority at feeding-time, when if allowed he chases Djoum and Mushie off their rightful food. To the relief of his companions, Richard now separates him for the evening meal. At the moment, Mumbah is trying to test his strength against the adult females but lacks the confidence to make much progress. Age and experience confer definite advantages in the status race, and sometimes it seems that older females present a united front against the upstart whom a few years ago they were carrying around on their backs and protecting from the ill-temper of Gugis. From our experience it is a hard grinding struggle for a black-back to climb up the rungs of the social ladder. He meets stubborn resistance at every level. Mumbah has to beat his way past Ju Ju and Baby Doll to be faced with Mouila and then Shamba. It will probably take him two more years to accomplish this, and having done so he will be staring into the cold amber eyes of Gugis and Kisoro. Mumbah will never make the grade of patriarch as his growth rate indicates that he is destined to weigh in at 300 pounds or less, far below the qualifying weight for that role. Though in excellent physical shape, he may have been held back in development by a complaint that was diagnosed as amoebic dysentery by the late Dr W. C. Osman Hill, the famous primatologist whose wisdom and experience were much appreciated on his frequent visits to Howletts. To counteract a loose stomach, which is a symptom of this disease, we have had to give him a daily dose of Kaolin. In spite of this, Mumbah is one of the most athletic and active of the colony and certainly takes first prize for game inventiveness. He was the first to teach himself to ride the cable reel, forcing it forward with his hands and keeping his balance, like an acrobat. He was also the first to use the trapeze effectively, using a hanging rope as a pulley to work up a swing.

Mumbah is the drummer of the band and has discovered every place in his enclosure that will serve his purpose: the shut-off slides, the chute-panels, the sheet metal roof and even the official drum itself. Of course every gorilla has a built-in drum in his own massive chest, provided as it is with special air-pockets to amplify the famous pok-a-pok-pok-pok. To our sorrow it seems that Mumbah is under-sexed. By now he should have attempted to copulate with the females or at least show some sexual interest and go through the motions. His genitalia, though small, are complete and it is possible that he is just a late developer. He has of course had ample opportunity to observe mating activity in the group and has no epicene, let alone effeminate, characteristics. Even at this age, my daughter Jamunda can still play with him but now prefers the company of Djoum, Mushie and the babies. The good thing about Mumbah is his honesty of mood. When he is jealous or challenging he lets us know it and we can take the necessary precautions. When in a good mood Mumbah can make a delightful companion. Spite, vindictiveness, treachery – all are foreign to his nature. He lacks size to a considerable degree and to a lesser extent, courage, but these are amply compensated for in the person of Djoum, the next male in the hierarchy.

Djoum at nine years and 178 pounds is a remarkable ape. I personally believe that he is the patriarch of the nineties. He has a special distinction easier to discern than to define. Where Mumbah will cower before Gugis in fear, Djoum will turn and face him. When cornered he will stand and fight, and Mumbah bears many marks on his chest and shoulders to confirm this. Self-confident, good-natured, he is the possessor of a life force that leaves one exhausted in his wake. When he arrived in 1969, accompanied by Mushie, he was one year old, pot-bellied and almost naked. He weighed 12 pounds and his hopes of survival seemed remote. My second wife, Min, mothered the infants, sleeping with them in her bed for the first six weeks, and somehow managed to accomplish the 'mother-image transfer' without which they could not have lived for long. Gorilla babies are far more dependent on love and attention than human ones. The mother ape will keep her child in unbroken physical contact for the first few months. They literally crave for affection and cannot be exiled to wards or dormitories or farmed out to day-nurseries. Like Schaller, I believe that the mother-infant bond can last for life, though we have no proof of this, as the first gorilla birth in captivity was only in 1954 (Columbus, Ohio) and most zoos are unable to keep enough members of a gorilla family together for long enough to provide a proper test.

Djoum, unlike Mumbah, is showing definite signs of sexual awareness. He has been seen going through the copulatory motions with Mushie, JuJu, and, on several occasions, with the mighty Shamba. Of course he is still far too young to be effective, but we are hopeful that in a few years Howletts will have a home-reared breeding male. Djoum is the most massively constructed of the juveniles, and his growth rate tells us that he is likely to be the largest of all our apes. We believe he will eventually reach well past the 400-pound mark. His physique stood him in good stead when, at the weight of eighty pounds, he fell twenty feet from the roof of the play run and landed heavily on his back on a wooden platform. Richard, who saw the accident, was amazed when Djoum righted himself, shook his head and carried on brachiating as if nothing had happened. On another occasion he got his foot caught in a hanging rope that had become shredded from constant use. The knot tightened as he struggled and there was nothing he could do but hang upside down until help arrived. When we found him we estimated that he had been suspended for over half an hour. In fifteen more minutes he would have hæmorrhaged from blood pressure to his head. On examination we found that a bone had been cracked in his heel, the whole area of which was grotesquely swollen. In two weeks he was back to normal and as active as ever. The fracture healed of its own accord.

Richard and I rate Djoum at least the equal of Gugis and Baby Doll in intelligence and certainly superior to Mumbah and Kisoro. If he has a future rival for the patriarchate it might prove to be Bitam, a six-year-old male who also seems set for great things. Of all the gorillas, Djoum seems to have the most marked sense of humour. Gorilla humour, as befits their warm nature, has no element of *schadenfreude*. They like to laugh in sympathy with you or in anticipation of a game they specially enjoy. In a certain mood if one even makes the movements which suggest a tickling bout they will start to laugh, even though one has not actually touched them. The game that sends Djoum into transports of delight is 'nip your little toe'. This must be a time-honoured favourite as it is known to all. Gorillas are hypersensitive in exactly the same places as humans, under the armpits and on the soles of their feet. The only one to tickle back regularly is Shamba. Unfortunately I am not ticklish, so when she starts rummaging my ribs I have to pretend to laugh. Djoum wrestles with Mumbah and suffers considerable punishment without a murmur of complaint. Their present daily bouts foreshadow the majestic jousting that is to come. It is a great rarity to see two adult male gorillas together in a zoo, but at Howletts we hope one day to run four in the same enclosure: Mumbah, Djoum, Bitam and Toumbi. Djoum has never been known to give a mean or ill-tempered bite, but his routine play-bites are quite painful, nor is he yet aware that his increasing weight makes some of his games almost intolerable. One of the problems of wrestling with male gorillas is that they treat you as one of themselves, a compliment that one could willingly do without when they are in an active mood. A gorilla is built on a scale and in a fashion that helps to render ineffective any blows that a man can level at him. His head is sunk into his shoulder-mass and the crest itself acts as a helmet, composed as it is of extended jaw muscle. A human, angular and vulnerable, is no match of any sort for him in friendly open combat. The eventual difference between male and female play is that the former, however good-natured, has a competitive quality. It is this factor, accentuated by the approach of maturity, that renders any intimate physical interaction between a human being and an adult male gorilla almost impossible. The only exception I know of was the extraordinary relationship between Stefi, the adult breeding male at Basle, and his keeper Stemmler. Stefi is especially easy-going and Stemmler was quite exceptional in his emotional rapport with his apes. We at Howletts are inspired by his exploits and intend to emulate them – if we can.

Mumbah and Djoum initiate the new types of play, the former being the more skilful operative, the latter the more enterprising and adventurous. When the new heated swimming-pool was installed, it was Djoum who first summoned the courage to plunge in. He subsequently became the water-baby of the group, thrashing about up to his waist. Mumbah and Mushie, along with the three juveniles, keep to splashing and paddling and skimming the surface on a rope. Gorillas, like humans, can be taught to swim, and this has been accomplished at Jos Zoo in Nigeria, where two apes have become proficient breast-strokers. The only instance of a self-taught swimming ape, to my knowledge, was the male orang-utan at Al Ain Zoo in Abu Dhabi. The zoo director, Otto Bulart, told me that his breeding male swam across a twenty-five-foot moat on three different occasions and escaped. The last time had tragic consequences as he died of sunstroke, Bulart, the only man who could handle him, being away at the time. Our adult gorillas show a limited interest in their pool, drinking from it and sometimes idly dabbling the water with their hands and feet. If one throws food that sinks to the bottom they will go after it and collect it without hesitation. Like us, they prefer the water to be over seventy degrees.

When one enters the gorilla enclosure, the choice of play partners is curtailed by the demands of hierarchy. In fact it is particularly easy to discern rank by studying the play order. I may wish to romp with Djoum, but will not be

allowed to if a senior ape has other ideas. The youngest trio are still excused from these severities on account of age, but have formed a firm rank-order of their own – Bitam–Founa–Toumbi. Mushie, at the age of seven, is the lowest in her sub-group, comprised of Mumbah, Djoum and herself. She is adept at holding her own and playing off one male against the other. If Djoum bullies her too much she knows that Mumbah will come thumping to her aid. If Mumbah threatens, Djoum will take her side. One of her peculiarities is hand-clapping, either self-taught or copied from the chimps. To her this activity seems a game, or at least an expression of good spirits, and to a lesser degree it has been observed in the others. Schaller believes that chest-beating, hand-clapping and other body noises serve to inform gorillas of each other's whereabouts, in the heavy cover of the forest, when even the distance of a few yards can mean visual separation.

Mushie is the most 'generous' of the gorillas, often making seemingly altruistic gifts from her food to me, and more often to my daughter Jamunda. Gugis has this habit also, but with him the intention is successful barter. He will push something through the mesh and wait for a tit-bit in return. In his younger days he would often expect me to chew certain items of his fare and then feed them back to him orally – a paedomorphic trait he abandoned with the advancing years. Mushie, on the other hand, will expect one to enjoy her offerings, though sometimes in the case of an apple or an orange she will take it back after a few bites. Of all the group she cries the most at the departure of her human friends, sometimes getting so perturbed that she will retch with emotion in chimp-like fashion, and bury herself in the straw face-downwards, like a human child in a tantrum. In a few years Mushie will be put to Kisoro and we see no reason why she should not breed successfully, though she will be lucky to attain a weight of much more than 150 pounds.

Already at the approximate ages of five to six the differing characters of the youngest trio can clearly be seen. Bitam at seventy-two pounds is six pounds heavier than Toumbi and has established a facile dominance over him and the solidly constructed Founa, a girl of about his own age but a few pounds lighter. Bitam is rougher than any of the other males was at his age, and seems destined to equal Shamba in gluttony. He downed so much of Toumbi's rations that the latter started to lose condition, and we now feed him his share personally from the hand. Bitam's favourite game is a rhythmic shoving or pulling, using one's knee or back as a sort of rocking-base. He can keep this up for some time and he occasionally gives climatic hoots when really excited, not unlike the sounds made by an adult male during orgasm. Possibly this behaviour is proto-sexual, as it is only provoked by an animate body. When we move the three youngsters each day from their sleeping nursery to the play pen, they have to walk along the corridor past the other apes. For this procedure they adopt the tandem position, Toumbi in front, Founa in the middle and Bitam bringing up the rear. This order has never varied and Richard remarked to me that he thought this surprising, as it was the reverse of their rank order. An explanation may lie in the habit of dominant male gorillas bringing up the rear when their band is under threat and they are trying to escape. Bitam is already protective towards Founa and looks likely to fall into his natural masculine roles in the future. The three, though often merged into the larger community, are virtually inseparable. Founa has a gentle and affectionate disposition almost devoid of aggression at this stage. Little Toumbi has come on a lot recently and has at last begun to revel in the joys of playing with human beings. He is very slow to give his trust, and only time, patience and love can win him over. He is without the brash confidence of Bitam, and is probably always destined to live beneath his shadow. His physical appearance is very similar to that of Gugis at the same age, and I hope to be able to live long enough to see his back turn silver in the middle eighties.

I feel I cannot do full justice to the fine breeding male Kisoro that Lincoln Park Zoo, Chicago, so kindly sent to us to make good where Gugis had failed, simply for the reason that I have known him for so short a time. Kisoro was wild-caught and arrived at Lincoln Park when he was two years old. He joined the Howletts band in September 1973, at the age of twelve, having already sired a son and a daughter from two separate females. At the time of writing, just over two years later, he has excelled this performance at Howletts: JuJu having been delivered on 2 April 1975 of a boy – Kijo – whom she is rearing most conscientiously; Shamba of a girl – Kimba – on the morning of 30 April 1975; Baby Doll of a boy – Kisabu – on 29 May 1975 and Mouila yet another boy – Koundu – on 6 October 1975. Kisoro's virility is astonishing, as his record to date makes him the father of six, all from different females and all, except Kisabu, alive and strong. He must be in the running for world champion stud captive gorilla, and he is certainly the first gorilla in history – and prehistory for that matter – to sire progeny on both sides of the Atlantic. At the moment his greatest rival is Jambo of Jersey Zoo, father of six.

Kisoro is the only adult male gorilla to have made the ocean crossing, west to east, and it says something for the enterprise and judgement of the Lincoln Park directorate that they could adopt this high-reward, high-risk stratagem. Kisoro seemed none the worse for his journey by air and he was accompanied

6. Bassa is introduced to Ju Ju 7. (over) *Mumbah*

Kisoro

by his friend and keeper, Jim Higgins, and his veterinary surgeon, Dr Erich Maschgan. The four adult females at Howletts accepted him quite readily after some preliminary bickering, and they all seem to find him more trustworthy and predictable than Gugis. He seems to have a more direct nature than Gugis, and this quality is reflected in the easy confidence that he inspires in the seraglio.

Kisoro is quite unperturbed by strangers entering his service corridor, and we put this down to his ten years' experience of a milling public in a great urban zoo. The only time he shows aggression towards his keepers is when food items that he wants are passed on to another gorilla. These apes are quarrelsome over food in captivity, where there is a limited supply, and they have not really developed a perfect social restraint to neutralise this tendency, because for tens of thousands of years the situation could never have arisen, the floor and understorey of the rain-forest being blessed with palatable fodder in sufficient abundance to preclude any competition. Dian Fossey, however, has noted that in the wild state gorillas *can* resent the close approach of another when feeding.

It is doubtful if Gugis and his supplanter, Kisoro, will ever meet face to face in the same enclosure, though such a confrontation, if ever filmed or televised, would make a spectacle that would put the antics of heavy-weight boxers to shame. My personal view is that not much would come of it as both are so evenly matched, Gugis giving away a few pounds in weight, but lacking Kisoro's supple agility. My money would be on Gugis if a real fight developed, as the home player starts with a marked advantage. It would be interesting to see how the females would line up if it came to a real showdown, and my belief is that their ancient ties with Gugis would supersede their sexual attraction to Kisoro, but in the event all four would not necessarily act in unison. If they did, the recipient of their wrath would be in bad trouble. At the moment, the two males vent their jealousy and spleen by displaying, strutting, and thumping the intervening mesh with shattering violence.

The summer of 1975 was an eventful one. Richard discovered JuJu's baby at 8 a.m. on 2 April, and believes that birth took place approximately an hour or so beforehand. To our joy, JuJu proved to be a most conscientious mother, and after some initial experimenting soon learned to hold the baby the right way up. Six hours after birth breast-feeding was observed and within a full day JuJu had the situation well in hand. At a guess, the baby, Kijo, weighed just over four pounds. On several occasions during the first few days following birth, JuJu cradled him in her right hand and performed masturbatory movements with his back against her vulva. I have never heard or read of similar behaviour before, and we were nonplussed as to its significance. However the association of a new-born infant with the genitalia is scarcely surprising. Only humans seem to have largely separated sexuality from reproduction, and a heavy price we have paid for this unfortunate experiment. Thirty hours after the birth I went in with JuJu and Kijo and presented her with two boiled eggs and some digestive biscuits. She was not perturbed by my presence and in a few days was even prepared to play with her keepers and with me. At twelve days we let the three juveniles, Bitam, Toumbi and Founa, in with the mother and baby. To begin with, great interest was shown by the trio, but on subsequent occasions Founa paid much more prolonged attention to the baby than either of the males, emphasising that the division of the roles between the sexes is evident from the earliest years. JuJu was obviously pleased to see the young ones and even allowed them to touch the baby on its head. JuJu has also had visits from her two friends, Mouila and Baby Doll. Mouila showed definite signs of tension which looked to us very like jealousy and she seemed to qualify these by displaying, strutting and the assertion of her old dominance. We therefore made a point of not leaving Mouila with JuJu without supervision in case of accidents. JuJu hardly took any notice of Baby Doll's presence when we put them together, and Baby Doll, after satisfying her initial curiosity with lengthy stares, ignored the mother and baby.

We have noticed that Gugis in the adjoining enclosure has reacted benignly to JuJu and Kijo. This has surprised us as he has always treated the appearance of a new ape with resentment. Certainly, it took about a year for him to accept Bitam, Toumbi and Founa in the cage next to him, even though they were only fifteen or sixteen months old and hardly posed any sort of threat to him. When Mouila was pushing her weight about, Ju Ju hurried to Gugis's corner for protection and was greeted by a welcoming grunt. JuJu has also made definite attempts to appease Kisoro through the mesh. Can it be that a mother gorilla feels the necessity to introduce the baby to the dominant males of her band at an early opportunity? This is borne out by Dian Fossey's studies in Ruanda. She notes that females with newly-born young stay as close as possible to the overlord for protection. Within three weeks of Kijo's birth, JuJu was also indulging in quite active games with myself and Richard. In fact she has seldom been more forthcoming since her childhood days, taking literally, I suppose, a new lease of life.

Twenty-eight days after Kijo's birth, which in itself was the most notable event recorded at Howletts, Shamba had a daughter, Kimba, on 30 April.

Ju Ju enjoys a beer

In spite of standing vigil at Ju Ju's parturition and witnessing all the subsequent maternal behaviour, Shamba showed no interest whatsoever in her baby, which came unexpectedly early in her gestation. After five hours of neglect, Kimba was removed and found to be quite cold. She weighed 3 lb 12 oz, slightly under-sized but otherwise in perfect shape. An incubator had been installed in Richard's house, and Kimba was moved forthwith to join a yearling chimpanzee female, Binkes, and a week-old honey badger kitten. Kimba is in appearance just like her mother and has inherited her gluttony, showing undisguised impatience at the approach of the bottle and petulance at its removal. Shamba's lack of interest in motherhood has disappointed us, but there are some examples of females taking up their second baby, even though ignoring their first. A possible mitigating factor in Shamba's case is the fact that she was ill after parturition and perhaps forgot her natural duties in her own suffering. The only advantage to be gained by her failure is that she will no doubt soon come back into oestrus and Kisoro should get her pregnant again within a year or so. In the normal course of events, births would be separated by three or four years.

On 29 May 1975, Baby Doll duly gave birth to a male, Kisabu. Richard found the baby in seemingly good shape at eight o'clock in the morning. Baby Doll made a great effort to mother her baby but after seventy-two hours we decided to take it away from her. From the first she showed it affection but seemed to regard it more as a treasured toy than a real live baby. She put it on her head, carried it in her thigh pit and sometimes left it alone for alarmingly long periods. Two breast-feeds were observed, but one was for less than a minute. Eventually she seemed to lose patience and tried to squeeze it through the bars for us, apparently, to take care of. This last behaviour convinced Tom Begg, Richard and myself that the whole exercise had become too much for her. The baby, whom we called Kisabu, did not seem in such bad shape but had some swellings on its left elbow and finger joints. We were worried by these but put them down at first to bruises from the cavalier handling he had received from his mother. He weighed 4 lb 3 oz and my wife Sally volunteered to look after him. In spite of the most meticulous care, he failed to put on weight and his swellings remained. We had him examined by a paediatrician, Gordon A. MacKinlay, and discovered that he was suffering from neonatal septicæmia with osteomyelitis and septic arthritis. He had contracted a streptococcus infection from his mother, whose vaginal membrane had burst a few days before birth thus setting up an infection which he carried to his death six weeks later. Baby Doll herself was in a bad way and we anæsthetised her for examination and for the extraction of some blood for her son. This proved to be of the right group and she herself recovered after treatment with Penicillin K given orally. Sally, with the dedicated help of Dr MacKinlay and Genevieve Bailey – a nurse specialising in the intensive care of premature babies – struggled for weeks to keep Kisabu alive, but all in vain. The reduction of the red corpuscles caused fatal wastage of his kidneys and the thrice-daily injections to counteract this weakened his resolve. The death of Kisabu cast a pall over everyone who had come to know him. It seemed amazing that even in six weeks a gorilla baby could generate so much love and affection.

Fortunately, Mouila's baby, which arrived on 6 October 1975, was no problem at all. I found him myself at 10.30 p.m., the very night we thought the

(left) *Kijo* (right) *Gugis at fifteen months with Jamunda, then two*

birth might take place. We had thought Mouila was due at least a month before and she had grown to an almost grotesque size. We even thought she might be having twins, an occurrence recorded only twice in captivity. On the morning of 6 October she looked queasy and kept herself away from all the others. She was also off her food and would not allow any of the juveniles to approach her. Richard, Peter, Tom Begg and I had arranged to look in every two hours through the night, and this time I was the lucky one to find the baby. Mouila proved to be a copy-book mother, taking skilled care of the infant, and it seemed to us that she must have learnt a great deal from Ju Ju's example.

We often put the two nursing mothers together and they indulge in the most heart-warming, bond-strengthening behaviour. Once, after a tiff, they ended up with each other's babies. Kijo, the elder, ran back to his mother and Ju Ju ended up with both. My daughter, Jamunda, who had witnessed the initial melee, was horrified by the turn of events, and Richard and I gave each other puzzled looks. Finally, we went in together to monitor the next moves. Mouila was clearly very worried at the loss of her infant and I decided to restore Koundu to her myself. Ju Ju showed no resentment at my interference but Mouila was demonstrably grateful when I placed her five-week-old son back in her arms.

64   (above) *Ju Ju and Mouila with their babies* (opposite) *Mouila and Koundou*

Once we had three healthy additions to the gorilla band we decided to take the risk and dope Gugis to find out whether he was impotent or infertile. The sexologists from the Wellcome Institute came down to take a semen test under the supervision of Tom Begg. Though we took blood samples and examined his teeth, which were perfect, the experts failed to coax the inert Gugis into ejecting any sperm. We did establish however that his testicles and penis were underdeveloped. In view of this we do not hold out much hope of breeding from a home grown male until Djoum looms into the picture in three or four years time.

I would not like to finish this chapter on the Howletts gorillas without paying tribute to those that have died since the founding of the colony in 1958. Tragedy struck in the late summer of 1967, just after I had returned from a trip to West Africa. On my return Derek Rushmer, Richard Johnstone-Scott's predecessor, told me that the great male, Kulu, who had arrived from Basle six years before at the age of five and had grown to a magnificent 320 pounds, was ill and wasted. I was appalled to see the deterioration that had set in during the month that I had been away. I knew he was dying, and dying fast. The two local agricultural veterinary surgeons had no idea what was the matter with him, and in spite of his drastic loss of condition, remained sanguine as to his chances. They had taken faecal and urine samples but had come up with nothing. Kulu had become a desiccated hulk and died four days later. Even during his death throes, the mighty ape's strength was such that he grabbed me when I was trying to give him a drink and bowled me over with a shove of his arm. A week after his death, an eight-year-old female, Dinghi, was struck down with the same complaint. Dinghi was the boon companion of Mouila and in the pink of condition. The autopsy on Kulu had revealed nothing and he had been buried at the end of the avenue. Dinghi worsened so rapidly that I had Kulu's body exhumed and re-examined for mineral poisoning. Nothing came to light and in despair we were compelled to watch another gorilla die before our eyes. I sent Dinghi's corpse to the Animal Health Clinic at the London Zoo and a post-mortem revealed a massive intestinal infestation of the parasite strongyloides. At an early stage of infestation this condition can be easily treated, so a diagnostic failure had precipitated a needless tragedy. In the period I had known him, Kulu had made a deep impression on me and all the gorillas. If he had lived, he would I am sure have made a noble patriarch and a productive one. He seemed to have in ample supply the qualities of a leader, and there is no doubt that his untimely loss set back the colony for a decade.

No sooner had we partially recovered from these terrible events than a similar

Kulu is dead,
His females look for him:
Mouila, Shamba, Baby Doll.
His power and strength
Were theirs – they loved him.

They lived beneath his arms,
Inside his brow-ridged gaze.
His great back,
Half-silver with half-age
Was their protection.

When darkness fell they knew
That he was there,
Restless and silent
With his padded hands
Until the dawn.

disaster struck us. On my travels in the Cameroons I had bought a two-year-old baby gorilla female from a mission station near Elolowa. She had been hand-reared by some priests and was one of the friendliest and highest-spirited little gorillas I had ever come across. A few months after her arrival at Howletts she began to ail and a form of thrush, or mouth fungus, was diagnosed. Treatment proved ineffective and knowing a young gorilla's incapacity to survive de-socialisation, I decided to put our most maternal adolescent female, Moundou, in with her, to keep her company and take care of her. The gamble failed, Moundou contracted this same rare form of stomatitis and both died within days of each other. These blows, one after the other, had crushed my careless optimism and left me with a feeling of guilt and inadequacy. I decided that if I was to carry on, I could no longer rely on the lack of specialist knowledge and faint commitment to my particular purposes of the local veterinary surgeons. For the last eight years, Howletts has had the services of a full-time resident veterinary surgeon and I am glad to say that – apart from Kisabu – there have been no further deaths in the colony since then.

Tigers

WHO can ever hope to describe the tiger in its beauty, in its pride? George Schaller, who spent many months in the Kanha reserve in India studying the tiger and its prey in preparation for his book *The Deer and the Tiger*, told me that the sight of his first tiger in the wild evoked in him wild imaginings. This great cat is the very stuff of legend and romance. His name is symbolic to us of ferocity, power and comeliness. The tiger occupies a position in Chinese and Indian culture close to that of the lion in the West. This has not prevented him being decimated throughout his range. The population in India is dwindling to below a thousand from an estimated 40,000 before the war. In South-East Asia, a further two thousand may still survive. In China the last few dozen still face a death penalty. There he is classed as vermin, an interesting and revealing term used by humans to describe the rightful owners of terrain they themselves have stolen or wish to steal. In the U.S.S.R. about a hundred snow-tigers survive in the Amur district of Siberia. In Iran the Persian tiger, the Hyrcanian tiger of the ancients, still subsists in the Caspian forests, but numbers are believed to be less than twenty. Professor Paul Leyhausen has told me that he had a pug-mark cast from Persia which was definitely tiger not leopard; but *Panthera tigris virgata* is certainly one of the rarest animals in the world. In captivity about a thousand tigers of all races are spreading throughout the world. At a guess, for every million humans there is one tiger. Ironically, if a tiger kills a human it has to die, in spite of the fact that it probably had no choice but theophagy – dining on a god – or death by starvation.

In the last fifteen months we bred over thirty tigers successfully at Howletts, twenty-one Indian and ten Siberian, from six different mothers. The colony is probably the largest in the world, though Leipzig, Kolmarden and Rotterdam also have large groups. Apart from the thirty-odd survivors, we lost three from a genetic malformation, four from accidental crushing by the mother or father and one from drowning in a torrential rainstorm. The input of Indian tigers at Howletts has been five animals, the output is now approaching seventy. The Siberian colony was only started five years ago, and its numbers have increased from seven to seventeen, ten successful births and one death. Curiously, we have only bred females from the giant race, and all from the same pair, Zarif and Gonza. Since going to press a further pair have bred successfully, Sukam and Gulya. Gulya gave birth to two cubs, a male and a female, on 20 June 1975 and all are doing well.

Zarif was the tiger chosen by the painter, David Shepherd, as a model for his famous portrait of a Siberian tiger, 'Tiger Fire', of which 850 prints were made and all sold for £150 each, the proceeds of which he most generously gave to 'Project Tiger'. Eric Tenney painted Zombie (an Indian tigress) with her two cubs, Gunga and Waitara. Ralph Thompson has spent more time with the tigers than any other artist, and his representation of 'Chuga', a huge male Siberian, is particularly faithful in capturing his 'honest' look.

The first tiger, or rather tigress, in my life was the beautiful Tara. She was sold from Edinburgh Zoo in 1958, and I found her in a pet store near Regent's Park. She was nine weeks old and cost me two hundred pounds. At the age of thirteen, Tara was killed by her mate Mazar, whom I had procured from an Austrian dealer when she was two years old. To compound the tragedy autopsy revealed three well-developed foetuses. At the time of writing over forty of her descendants are alive, twenty-two of them at Howletts. Tara was a mind-opener for me. We raised her on the bottle and she slept in my bed for the first eighteen months. So sound was her character and so sweet and affectionate her nature that I supposed at first I had an exceptional animal on my hands. Experience subsequently told me that her qualities were typical of her species. To some extent I must have been suborned by the age-old propaganda against the tiger, because I remember being surprised that she never bore malice or resentment. Instinctively a man strikes back if he is hurt by a claw or a bite, and when I first cuffed her in annoyance at some pain, she hissed and bared her fangs. A few minutes later the incident was forgotten, and slowly, as time went by, she learnt to play with retracted claws and restrained teeth. Though agreeably disposed towards mankind in general, she was not prepared to put up with any

Zombie, who has become the mother of many, with two of her earliest cubs

8, 9. All tigers enjoy water and are excellent swimmers. Although I am a strong swimmer, Zemo, the 'diving tiger' can easily outpace me in the water. Diving came easily to him, but unlike humans he dives not for amusement but to retrieve something. On occasions he will swim to the bottom of the pool with his eyes open like a seal

10. (over, above) *Zarka the one-eared and Zola mating in the snow. Zarka was the first tiger to be born at Howletts and his mother chewed off his right ear, perhaps mistaking it for the umbilical cord*

11. (over, below) *Mazar killing Daisy. We believe this to be a unique photograph*

12. (over, opposite) *A Siberian tigress and her cub*

familiarities from outsiders. My butler panicked one lunch-time when Tara was idly playing with his foot, and he lashed out at her with a savage kick. After this incident, Tara released such terrifying growls of anger whenever he appeared that he gave his notice.

Though always suspicious of the tiger lore to be found in the old hunting books, I had to some extent succumbed to its influence. Fortunately Eardly Wilmot and Champion had long ago provided me with a more acceptable rendering of the tiger's behaviour and character. Even Corbett, the famed tiger-slayer, had come to admire the nature of this cat, even referring to him as a 'gentleman'. Certainly the raising of Tara from a cub of two months to an adult swept away many cobwebs. The first to go was the belief that a tiger cub becomes less reliable and affectionate when it progresses from a milk to a meat diet. The next to disappear was the myth that a tiger will get excited at the smell of fresh blood from an open wound. My experience here was that Tara used to lick a gash with beneficial effect. I have observed this behaviour between siblings and adults. Any small injuries seem to heal much quicker for this attention. Another popular story is that tigers 'revert' to a supposedly pristine state of ferocity at the threshold of adulthood. This, of course, is far from the mark, as their natural condition is one of lazy indifference or good nature. My extensive experience of many tigers has proved that even extreme hunger fails to dispel their trust and love of man once given and once earned. When Tara had her first cubs I was chary of entering her breeding den, which was only 12 ft × 6 ft. Popular belief, perpetuated by the reminiscences of numerous Shikaris, had left a lingering doubt in my mind as to the nature of my welcome. A tigress in the presence of her cubs was supposed to be ferocity incarnate. When I entered her den she purred in recognition, and one of her whelps crawled towards me complaining bitterly. I picked it up to sex it and it screamed in alarm. Tara's reaction was to bring the other baby over for my inspection. The first cub was a male, Zemo, who later became the diving champion.

My relationship with Tara was so extraordinary that I began to think that she was atypical, a prodigy of goodwill and generosity. However the opposite was the truth. Of all the tigers that have been bred at Howletts, now numbering over sixty, only two or three show a deviant or treacherous nature. Probably a mean average among the high mammals, excepting man and other domestic animals. In the case of man aberrant behaviour has almost become the norm, through grotesque over-crowding accompanied by ineffectual socio-political controls. The tiger remains a solid citizen. Contrary to the accepted view, many

13. Zea, a Siberian tigress, taken at night

male tigers make indulgent fathers, and we have several breeding pairs that we leave together permanently. In the wild state the pregnant tigress would probably first weigh up the character of her mate before deciding to hide up. A good male no doubt has his uses, particularly in the provision of food and protection of the lair from man, hyaena, wild dog, and jackals. Few zoos to my knowledge exhibit tigers in family groups as we do at Howletts. It is an edifying sight.

On occasion guests have asked me whether feeding tigers helps to buy their friendship. This idea is once again far from the truth. First, I never personally feed the tigers, and second the attitude of a hungry tiger towards the purveyor of its food is closer to annoyance than gratitude. When a tiger sees his friend, the keeper, staggering towards him with a 70-pound haunch of beef, he is apt to regard that meat as his of visual right. What he sees is his prey and what he sees he owns. It is to be defended at all costs, in some cases even the final one. Some have even been known not to retreat from a fresh kill before the advance of an armed party. One of the first unpleasant lessons tiger cubs have to learn is never to approach an adult when feeding, not even their own mother – I have often witnessed a feeding tigress cuffing at her own hungry whelps, forcing them to wait until she herself is replete. This discipline is vital for their survival, but the discomfiture of the cubs is painful and even comic to watch. However friendly and trustworthy a tiger may be, none of us would dare approach one at first feed. Such an action would be interpreted as a challenge no tiger could afford to ignore. This state of mind is thrown into bolder relief at Howletts as we only feed the great cats once a week on average.

At Howletts we feed the tigers once a week in the summer and once every four days during the winter. This ties in with their natural customs. Most zoos feed their big cats every day, but this is to please the public, not the animals. 'Feeding Time at 3.30 p.m.' is a bad sign to read in a zoo if it refers to lions or tigers, as psychologically, these great predators are ill-fitted to daily feed-shifts. Contrast is as important to a tiger as it is to a human. Hunger followed by satiation, cold by warmth, solitude by company, these provide a backdrop that alone can make life bearable for a mammal.

The importance of his kill to a tiger cannot be exaggerated. A human or a herbivore is conditioned to a plentiful and permanent supply of food. The tiger is forced by circumstance to be a gambler, and however skilful he may be he needs luck on his side. To some extent he is at risk every time he strikes. Water-buffalo and gaur, the giant Indian forest ox, have accounted for many tigers; even sambar stags and wild swine are formidable adversaries. Nothing is easy

74   *Zemo with Zola and their three new-born cubs*

for a great carnivore, and well he knows it. A kill is ten days of contentment to a tiger.

The secret of gaining a tiger's love is to lay out the same commodity in lavish supply. There are many hand-reared tigers throughout the world, but most of these animals become intractable. The bottle is not enough on its own. The cubs must be loved to the same degree that a mother loves her child. Anything less will inflict half-tame animals on a zoo – the most awkward of all and the most dangerous. The love that is needed cannot come to order: it has to be there welling up from within. It must on no account be allowed to pupate into dominance. Dominance, if extended into maturity, has caused many tragedies and is not worth anything to a lover of big cats, who, with the exception of lions, are by nature independent and solitary, and not used to acceding to a superior authority.

We have learned at Howletts that very strong smells unsettle a tiger, particularly that of alcohol. Nick Marx suffered a severe mauling from a previously reliable tiger, Hoogli, when 'merry' with drink. He bears terrible scars on his left arm from this mishap. On another occasion at Howletts, the two keepers, Kurt Paulich and Brian Stocks, entered an enclosure of five adult Indian tigers, Jhelum, Indus, Putra, Bhima, Tapti. They had not been fed for fourteen days. The season was mid-summer when we have great difficulty procuring enough fallen stock. (Owing to a vagary in the English law, animals that die on a farm are not accepted as fit for human consumption. Hence the market price falls by ninety per cent, providing us with an economic supply of meat for our ninety carnivores.) Paulich was mildly drunk and three of the tigers, Jhelum, our largest Indian male (weight 420 pounds), Bhima and Tapti his sisters, pounced on him and he completely disappeared from sight under a growling, snarling trio of hungry cats. Brian Stocks hauled the tigers off his prostrate friend and helped him to his feet. He was amazed to find only one slight graze on Paulich's neck. An astonishing escape and one that says much for the self-control of these carnivores. Both keepers were shaken and the lesson went home. Indus and Putra took no part in the assault.

I have had a few unpleasant moments with tigers. Jhelum once threatened me and I felt an almost trance-like numbness steal upon me. This did not prevent me making a dignified exit in good time. David Livingstone recorded a similar experience with a lion.

> Growling horribly close to my ear, he shook me as a terrier-dog does
> a rat. The shock produced a stupor similar to that which seems to be
> felt by a mouse after the first shake of the cat. It caused a sort of

dreaminess, in which there was no sense of pain or feeling of terror, though I was quite conscious of all that was happening. It was like what patients, partially under the influence of chloroform, describe, who see all the operation, but feel not the knife. This singular condition was not the result of any mental process. The shake annihilated fear, and allowed no sense of horror in looking round at the beast. This peculiar state is probably produced in all animals killed by the carnivora; and, if so, is a merciful provision by our benevolent Creator for lessening the pain of death.

I am inclined to agree with the view that prey animals are to some extent anæsthetised by fear when they succumb to predators, in a state possibly not dissimilar to the *ivresse de profondeur* familiar to deep-sea divers. The fear inspired by the great predators is indeed a classic phenomenon. It no longer bears any relation to the likelihood of injury or death among humans. This great fear is part of our race memory and is evoked by any well-publicised accident involving a great mammal, or by the news of an escape. 'Tiger Loose' or 'Gorilla Loose' are headlines that will take a populace back ten thousand years in a moment. For aeons we lived in awe of wild animals who were, some of them in a real sense, our competitors, during the hunting and pastoral periods. An average of one person in this country is killed by a wild animal per annum – usually a keeper – compared with an average of two killed by dogs, seven by domestic bulls and seven thousand by cars. Some years ago, when a girl's arm was severely mauled by tigers that had recently arrived at Howletts from

Amga becoming annoyed with Kurt Paulich

Canada, the incident was reported in the national press and even as far afield as Texas and Australia. The same day fifty-five people in Britain died from other accidents, domestic, industrial and on the road. Not one got a mention. The great mammals are uppermost in our subconscious mind, a fact well known to the advertising profession. 'Put a Tiger in your Tank' was the most successful advertisement ever. I wonder for how long after they are all extinct will the ad-men go on selling 'Jaguar' cars, 'Cheetah' tyres and 'Polar Bear' mints? Fairy tales and legends from deep antiquity tend to ensure that animals retain a primal place in our psyche. 'Little Red Riding-Hood', 'Who's Afraid of the Big Bad Wolf?', 'Goldilocks and the Three Bears' – the origin of these and many other nursery legends are lost in the mists of time.

Few animals have suffered such a character assassination as the tiger and few animals have warranted it less. The human race would have benefited more to see him as a paradigm rather than a rival. Better to sit on the apex of a faunal pyramid like the tiger than to perch in lofty isolation like St Simeon Stylites on a pillar after the fashion of man. The character and disposition of a tiger can vary to the same extent as that of a man or a gorilla. As each animal has a known hunting range which it demarcates and protects for as long as its food supply lasts out, its personality becomes known to the other inhabitants of the area, including humans. There are bold tigers and timid ones, honest tigers and treacherous ones, predictable and unpredictable, noisy and silent, hot-tempered and good-natured. From my experience of seventy animals in captivity, about one in twelve is delinquent to varying degrees, though we have not experienced a really aberrant animal.

We have found that animals that are untrustworthy in their conduct towards us are similar in their behaviour towards other tigers. The founding father of the Howletts colony, Mazar, was one of these, but fortunately, of all his off-spring, only his first daughter Zsa Zsa proved unreliable. Both Mazar and Zsa Zsa caused havoc among the other animals, Mazar killing no less than three of his tigresses – Kya, Tara, and Daisy. We believe Kya was killed while mating, when her son Zarka was three months old and being hand-reared. She was a weak tigress, and a post mortem showed that she was suffering from enteritis. Through Zarka the One-Eared, however, her bloodline survived. Tara, whom Ernst Lang described as one of the most beautiful tigresses he had ever seen, met a sticky end. She had always handled Mazar with consummate skill, mating with him and generally protecting herself from his occasional frustrated rages. It seems that some tigers become ill-tempered when they wish to copulate and the female is unreceptive or pregnant. Tara knew all

Chuga once suffered a bad attack of colic and we were able to relieve his pain by   79
massage. When he was too ill to leave the cabin, Kurt would climb in with him

about Mazar's bad habits, and would hole up in her den or take refuge on a ramp, facing his half-hearted threats with counter-threats. In the winter of 1970, however, it rained to such a degree that her enclosure became a sea of mud, and we started to build a large new enclosure for her, but one morning a few days before we had planned to move her we found her dying with her windpipe pierced – no doubt by one of Mazar's canines. She was covered in mud – having fought with Mazar and slipped. Unable to protect herself Tara then received her fatal wound. Autopsy showed three well-developed foetuses. I wept when she died, and buried her at the end of the lime avenue with my daughter Mameena, who died at a few months of age from a congenital heart fault. When moved by my grief at the loss of so close a friend I wrote the poem 'My Tigress'. It was some, but small, consolation to know that Mazar also felt the loss. He called for her every night for three weeks after her death. Her kind and loyal nature was bequeathed to most of her descendants. She did not live in vain, and if fortune smiles her genes will be much in evidence in the centuries to come, as ten of her offspring survive, eight of whom have bred.

Mazar's other crime was extraordinary. I had purchased a tigress who went by the trite name of 'Daisy'. She was experienced in raising her own young, and I wished her to impart this culture to my small group of females. Daisy arrived from Florida and during her six months of quarantine I placed her in the enclosure next to Mazar with whom I intended to mate her. After the statutory period we let them run together. Mazar dashed up to Daisy and pounced on her as if she was a nilghai cow. He caught her by the throat and in a few minutes she was dead from suffocation. Knowing something of Mazar's dossier we were not entirely unprepared. We dashed in, clanging dustbin lids like tambourines, and laid about Mazar with a spade. It was all to no avail. Nothing would deter him from his task. It was not a fight but an execution. The resident male tiger saw Daisy more as an interloper than as a prospective mate. After this disaster we rarely put a tigress with Mazar, particularly as by now his sons Zarka and Zemo had reached breeding age.

My Tigress, My Tigress, My Tigress,
When I hear Mazar's mournful cries
I can see the rufus red of your coat
And the white that surrounded your eyes.

I can hear your welcoming Tiger's purr
That only a Tiger can make,
And feel the caress of your Tiger's fur
Against my tear-stained face.

I swear to you now my Tigress
Your offspring shall live on
Through Zsa Zsa, Zombie and Zola,
Through Zemo and Zorra and Zon.

I swear it, I swear it, I swear it
To expiate man's basest crime
I shall increase your tribe to a thousand
Then join you in the jungles of time.

After the tiger colony was well established we decided to introduce some fresh genes. For this purpose we procured Benjy, whose name we Indianised to Bhenji. He was a young circus reject of about nine months. He came to us with a loathing and terror of the human race. Within eighteen months he had become one of the easiest of all in temperament. Bhenji was of a light yellow colour and distinguished by a mane worthy of a Serengeti lion. He is the only tiger I have ever seen with this characteristic. In the winter when his mane grew seven or eight inches long he had the appearance of a 'tigon' – offspring of male tiger and lioness. Unfortunately he was one of the two tigers to have died of disease in the life of the colony. He succumbed to nephritis but not before impregnating Zorra successfully. She gave birth to one male and three female cubs six weeks after his untimely death. Bhenji's son Zinjh looks exactly like him.

I am often asked whether there is any noticeable difference of temperament between the huge Siberian race and the Indian. At Howletts we have not observed anything of note. The conventional wisdom is that the further south

Assault by five Indian cubs

you go, the more fiery the temper, the more volatile the mood of the tiger. At Howletts we have kept only the Siberian and Indian races: the latter have undoubted Malay and/or Sumatran blood through Mazar, who carried this strain. This one could tell from his appearance which was short, thick-set, with a concave, well-whiskered head, and a coat with close-set stripes that sporadically merged into spots. The so-called Royal Bengal has become a term used indiscriminately for any Indian race of tigers. Most tigers kept in zoos that are not pedigreed as Siberian, Sumatran or Chinese are sub-race hybrids. Into this category falls the Howletts group. All tigers are closely related, the original race evolving in the vast *taiga* forests of eastern Siberia and dispersing comparatively recently as far west as the Caspian and as far south as Bali. Early Indian writings make frequent mention of the lion and scarcely refer to the tiger. The tiger probably invaded India within the last four thousand years and worked its way south through Burma, Malaya and Sumatra. Even quite wide stretches of sea water failed to deter the advance of this highly successful and modern predator. They have been known to swim great distances, and have adapted to a semi-aquatic life in the floating islands of the Ganges delta – the Sunderbans. All tigers are natural swimmers and I can personally confirm that they can easily outdistance a man in the water. Zemo, the second male reared at Howletts and Tara's first son, is a skilled diver (see colour plate 8). When he dives he does so in order to catch something he is chasing, not for the mere fun of it. When he was chasing me in the water he would even follow me down to the bottom

Chara, the first female Siberian tiger to be born in England.
Here she is ten days old

of the pool like a seal. Though a strong free-styler, Zemo could catch me with the greatest ease (see colour plate 9). I soon learned to avoid this occurrence as a tiger ducking is no joke. Zemo seemed unaware of the laws of respiration, and I was unable to hold my breath long enough really to enjoy this particular game. The tiger readily eats fish and like the jaguar, given the opportunity, soon becomes proficient at catching them. He seldom makes the classic human error of exposing the full potential of his abilities unless he has to in order to survive. If circumstances force him to become a cattle-lifter or a man-eater he will draw on reserves of caution and cunning scarcely credible in the normal conduct of his affairs. The great cats seldom make the mistake of being cleverer than they have to be.

In man, of course, tigers have found their nemesis. There is nothing they can do to adapt to him as he sweeps away the very cover that – along with prey and water – is a prerequisite of their existence. The cover is never replaced, domestic cattle take over from the wild deer and antelope and the water-table falls as the process of deforestation dries up lakes, rivers and streams. The tiger has one last card to play before he bows out for ever. He has the capacity to arouse in us admiration and affection. Were his nature and quality known to enough of us, his future would be assured. It is to be hoped that the growing band of his supporters throughout the world will remember him in the hour of his need. Could an animal of such immortal fame be allowed to pass from the earth? Is it possible that we will slowly watch him die without stirring from our stupor? If my words help to find for him a dozen friends, they will not have been written in vain – but such is his predicament that only a mass reversal of sentiment can hope to save him.

A mock chase by a group of one-year-old Indian tigers

Other Animals

THOUGH I have concentrated much of my attention in this book on gorillas and tigers I would not like the reader to think that I hold the other animals in my custody in less regard. One does of course have favourites among species and among individuals, and it would be idle to pretend that gorillas and tigers are not among the very forefront of the creatures which I admire and respect the most. Many of the great mammals at Howletts simply have not been with us long enough for me to give them the prominence they deserve. The elephants and rhinoceroses, for instance, are still too young to breed, and one day I would like to devote a whole book to them alone. The snow and Amur leopards, two of the rarest and most beautiful cats in the world, have scarcely settled down since their arrival from Chicago and Frankfurt respectively. Nothing much is known about either cat in the wild state. Unlike the clouded and the Amur varieties, the snow leopard or 'ounce' has recently been photographed for the first time, in its natural habitat, by George Schaller for the *National Geographic Magazine*, a truly remarkable achievement. In the near future we plan to establish breeding groups of these ultra-rare cats and so give them a helping hand to survive. Our original clouded leopard pair have successfully produced twelve infants over the last four years, but a further ten have been lost through disturbance and weather conditions. We have sent a pair to West Berlin and to Londrina in Brazil, and plan to send another pair to San Francisco in 1976.

Perhaps the greatest piece of luck we have had was to breed the African honey badger for the first time, in captivity, in the world. I first read about this

14. (over) *Indian elephant 15. Yearling male wolf shedding its winter coat*

extraordinary little animal in F. W. Champion's book, *The Jungle in Sunlight and Shadow*. He claimed from his own experience, and quoting Dunbar Brander and Captain Pitman, that the honey badger was the bravest animal in the world. I determined one day to befriend and breed this species but I never managed to get more than one of the Indian variety, so settled in the end for a pair I bought from a dealer in Windhoek, South-West Africa. Everything I had ever read about them proved almost an understatement. Though not aggressive without reason, they react to what they consider a threat by the hardest option of all – direct assault. I once took my Indian ratel for a walk with a three-quarters-grown tiger, Zarka. I bitterly regretted it, as the badger attacked the tiger and I got a severe bite from him as I went in to separate them. He was so furious at being pulled off Zarka that he literally turned round in his skin and bit me in the arm, in spite of the fact that I was holding him at arm's length by the loose scruff of his neck. Several babies have been born to our African group but only three have survived, the first of which was Tsumis.

The first animal I acquired is still with me, Dheddi, a black-capped capuchin monkey male. He was in a sorry state when I saw him in a pet store in the spring of 1957 – covered in sores and bald patches. I estimated his age at about a year and bought him out of pity for his condition and admiration for the spirit that illumined his frightened, but courageous, little eyes. He is now the father of seven living sons and two daughters, and the overlord of a clan numbering fourteen. It took months of assiduous attention to win over Dheddi's trust. His mother had probably been shot and his first experience of the human hand was to feel himself being wrenched from her stiffening body and plunged into a small crate ready for the dealer. Poor Dheddi! At first, progress was painfully slow but our relationship had one factor going for it – his brilliant intelligence. He soon divined, I suspect, my good intentions but was at the mercy of his mercurial temperament. The year before I bought Howletts I rented a charming country house near Abingdon in Berkshire, for two months in the summer, and had settled in there with my first wife, two Himalayan bears and Dheddi. A crucial test came when Dheddi escaped, only five weeks after I had bought him. He dashed out of an open window and along a garden fence out of sight into a spinney. I followed him gloomily wondering how I could ever hope to catch him again. I saw him soon in a dead apple tree, surrounded by a sea of fierce nettles. He was giving the clik-a-clok, clik-a-clok alarm call. I approached the tree and stood looking at him. I tried to reassure him with the gentle repetition of his name. I could sense that he was more frightened of the strange environment than he was of me. He made several

(above) *Tsumis, believed to be the first Honey Badger ever to be raised in captivity* (below) *Dheddi, my first animal*

movements in my direction but could not bring himself to make contact. After a long wait I decided on a stratagem. I started back to the house as if deserting him. He screamed in dismay, his eyebrows moving back and forth in alarm, after the fashion of his kind. I stopped and returned to the tree but this time I turned my back on him, as I had a feeling that an eyeball-to-eyeball confrontation was too much for him. This clinched it. He climbed on my shoulders, wrapped his prehensile tail round my neck and buried his head in his abdomen. So began a lasting friendship.

I found a beautiful girl for him three or four years later, called Shadow, and together they have founded a genuine little band of 'black-caps'. The heir-apparent, Nothing, is now twelve years old and looks exactly as his father looked at that age. Dheddi could live for many more years. At the San Diego Zoo, California, a black-cap male, Irish, lived to the age of forty-five and sired nineteen children. As the years progressed I have also established colonies of white-fronted capuchins and woolly monkeys which are now breeding well.

I procured my first chimpanzee when I was in New York in 1959. During my visit I won a few thousand dollars at Yonkers race track and the following day I went to Trefflich's animal store to buy something with my winnings. There, I encountered for the first time another life-long friend, a twelve-pound little chimp girl of the black-face variety whom we subsequently called Yonkus. She was in shocking condition and regarded my wife and me as saviours from the start. We had a problem at the Hotel Gotham, where we were staying, as we knew that the management would not permit a guest to keep a wild animal. We surmounted this by swaddling Yonkus from head to foot in expensive cashmere shawls and pretending she was a human baby. The ruse worked beautifully on the reception staff but not on the room maids, who had to be silenced by bribes. We booked Yonkus on the Pan Am flight home as a baby, as we knew she would not survive the further alienation of being crated and sent live-freight. The plan nearly came unstuck as we mounted the ramp to enter the plane. We were both loaded with the appurtenance of young motherhood to help allay any suspicions, and one of the stewardesses implored my wife to draw aside the shawl to see the face of a baby of such handsome parents! We explained that 'baby' was in a deep sleep and should not be disturbed – which was only too true as Yonkus had been given a sleeping pill to keep her quiet. Once we were in the air, the deception could be maintained no longer. Most of the passengers in the small first-class compartment were not amused – the captain of the plane even less so – but the affair was 'fait accompli' and there was nothing anyone could do about it.

Dheddi and Shadow, with Nothing just visible on her back

Yonkus lived to mother a son, Bongo, and two daughters, Binkus and Yonkus II, by the superb male, Bustah, whom we procured for her three years after her arrival at Howletts. She reared Bongo, but for some mysterious reason had no milk for Binkus, whom Richard had to rear himself. She had another baby last year and once again after leaving the infant with her for fifty hours we decided to remove it as yet again no milk had appeared. At this point tragedy struck. Tom Begg gave Yonkus the same knock-out dose as we had used before in the extraction of Binkus and this time she never came round. We were all quite shattered. She had become the matriarch of the chimp band and Richard and I were deeply attached to her. If we had guessed she was in any danger we would have left the baby to take its chance. As it happens, Yonkus II is doing very well and looks exactly like her mother.

Though extremely closely related to gorillas, chimpanzees provide a remarkable contrast with the larger ape. Emotionally the two species are poles apart and this difference is emphasised by much of their behaviour. Chimps are noisy creatures and Vernon Reynolds in his study *Budongo* puts forward the plausible theory that loud vocalisations are essential for a frugivorous ape. The gorilla occupies the primal biotope of the forest floor where a profusion of roots, pith and leaves provide him with an almost limitless abundance of forage. The chimp on the other hand, preferring fruit and kernels, depends on finding them when they are duly ripe. Reynolds and Goodall have witnessed many occasions when the loud hooting of the chimps who have just discovered ripe fruit has drawn in animals from miles around. Assemblies of up to eighty have been seen enjoying a feast of wild figs or marula. Chimps have competition from the highly adaptive baboons or drills that share their range. The lesser ape wears his heart on his sleeve. He has a low emotional threshold and is given to overt demonstrations of love and hate. Tantrums, which are seldom witnessed with gorillas, and then usually in the case of infants, are a regular feature of chimp behaviour. These attributes, plus a tendency to imitate man in his presence, invite us to look down on the chimpanzee. Most people feel superior to them and it almost seems that the species itself is prepared to cede the point. Of course most zoos exhibit juveniles only and few of the general public have ever studied a 180-pound adult male. If they did, their feeling of superiority might diminish as he presents a very impressive spectacle, particularly when 'displaying'.

Contrary to popular belief, there is not a discernible difference in intelligence between gorillas and chimps, though it is now conceded that the orang-utan is well behind both. Yerkes Primate Institute has completed I.Q. tests on the

Considerable success has been achieved at Howletts in breeding rare cats. All that are old enough to breed, except the cheetah, have done so and our next ambition is to raise snow leopards and Amur leopards from our two young pairs

16. Rimau, the black panther male

17. (Over, left) *Serval cat, the only cat that can run down its prey, apart from the cheetah. The servals at Howletts are breeding well.*

18. (Over, right) *The lynx was an inhabitant of the British Isles till about 1500 years ago. The Howletts pair were born in Marwell Zoo, Hampshire and have now bred for the first time*

19. (Opposite page 97) *Certainly one of the rarest and most secretive of all cats, the clouded leopard can claim to be the most beautiful as well. At Howletts we are now breeding the second generation, so our colony seems secure at last*

two apes and though chimps prove more proficient in manipulative skills, the gorillas were well up to the mark in conceptual thought. Sandy Harcourt, who studied the mountain race for two years with Dian Fossey, told me that he believed gorillas to have more persistence than the chimpanzee in completion of a task. These findings tie up with my own experience. The chimp appears to get a clear lead because he is more eager to learn and imitate. He is quicker, more willing and excitable. The gorilla, on the other hand, tends to take in everything but give little away. He would be a much finer poker player than the chimpanzee, keeping his cards close to his mighty chest.

I remember that Gugis and Shamba, when they lived with us in the cottage, would often watch us use the telephone, with no visible sign of interest; but one day I heard the staccato sound of conversation from the next room and saw Shamba holding the earphone in the right position. I thought she had answered the telephone, and picked up the receiver to enquire who was speaking. A flustered voice answered that he had just *received* a call and what was it all about? Lamely, I informed him that he had been dialled by a gorilla, he gave an uneasy laugh and hung up. Shamba had somehow managed to dial the three numbers necessary to get a local subscriber and the response that she had achieved spurred her on to more ambitious efforts. After this incident we had to lock the telephone in a cupboard.

Gorillas and chimps seem to get along very well in the rain-forest, a policy of avoidance being the general rule. I was informed by the hunting tribes near Kribi and Ebolowa in the Cameroons, that chimps sometimes drive away gorillas with clubs. I greeted these tales with undisguised disbelief but thought twice when I read Kortlandt's report on chimps. Kortlandt saw chimps attack an animated stuffed leopard with clubs and missiles – quite effectively at that. From my experience, gorillas are just as prone to use tools as their chimp cousins, and anyway what adaptive purpose would be served by antagonistic behaviour between gorillas and chimps? My personal guess would be that chimps would give way before an advancing gorilla band, though who knows what extraordinary incidents have passed unnoticed in the endless chronicles of the primal forest?

Numbers are a vital factor in the faunal dominance of high mammals. Five hyænas will drive off a leopard from a fresh kill, ten or a dozen will sometimes contend with a lion. No single tiger in its right mind would challenge an adult water-buffalo or gaur bull unless driven to desperation by hunger. Two, or preferably three, lions are needed to subdue an African buffalo bull. James Allen, for a long time warden of Seronera in the Serengeti, told me that he once saw twenty-six hyænas drive away three lions from a zebra kill. It is quite possible that a chimp clan of thirty to forty would disperse a small gorilla family. John McKinnon reports in his book *In Search of the Red Ape* of a family of large black gibbons or siamangs harrying and finally getting the better of a group of Sumatran orang-utans, forcing them to abandon a prized durian tree laden with heavy fruit.

I have to admit, and here I speak for myself alone, that in spite of all their admirable qualities I cannot quite summon the same respect and regard for the chimp as I so readily extend to the great gorilla. The reason for this, I think, is that I like to look up to great mammals. Chimps are too close to us in temperament and disposition. They invite condescension. English people of my background have been brought up to disdain excitability and emotional volatility. The poor old chimp is saddled with both and will never qualify for Rousseau's role of Noble Savage.

An animal that long ago captured my admiration by its very courage and aggression was the black rhinoceros. I have always longed to breed this species and in the summer of 1975 I observed that our six-year-old male, Baringo, was attempting to mount Rukwa, who is eighteen months his junior. Baringo was born in Dublin and came to Howletts when he was two years old. Only six or seven black rhino are born yearly, on average, in world zoos, so our satisfaction will be enormous if Rukwa or the other cow, Naivasha, gives birth during the next few years. The whole thing is a long process as the gestation period is eighteen months, and a female is unlikely to conceive until her sixth or seventh year.

It is a really exhilarating experience to 'go in' with black rhino because they are highly pugnacious animals. Of our group of three, Rukwa is the only one with an absolutely dependable character. Whatever happens, she remains calm and collected. Naivasha, of whom she is deeply fond, is crazily excitable. Both she and Rukwa were wild-caught and Naivasha bears a scar the size of a soup plate on her flank – possibly the work of a lion or the result of an accident when she was being roped. Either way, she is so nervous still that nothing much can be done with her. We even doubt if she is steady enough to allow Baringo to mount her. At the moment all his attentions are concentrated on Rukwa, and it will be a tragedy if Naivasha can never bring herself to accept him. I have seen black rhino mating in the Ngorongoro, and a noisy business it is. From the squeals and gyrations I thought at first I was witnessing a fight rather than a love-making.

The breeding of rhino in captivity is not an easy business as the male likes to

be unsighted from the female for some of the time. It is necessary to have the enclosure and paddocking on different levels or to erect heavy screening. Out of sight, out of mind, has a literal interpretation in rhino behaviour. Certainly with the small group at Howletts, Baringo the bull either seeks or avoids the company of the two cows, Rukwa and Naivasha. When he is 'stuck' with them against his inclination he vents his annoyance by blowing percussive curses at them and seeing them off. Sometimes he behaves in a similar fashion with me. An aggressive mood will come upon him and he will lower his head until his horn scrapes the ground, and blow at me through his nostrils. This threat is always effective in my case, though rarely exercised once he has accepted my presence for a caress, a scratch down or a soaking with the hose. Baringo's moods are clearly signalled and bad accidents should easily be avoided. When he does charge, however, he goes through with it and on several occasions I have had to vault the fence in undignified haste. Rukwa has never tried a threat of any sort, but Naivasha is a very different customer, predictably nervous and highly strung. She once caught me unawares but failed to go through her charge – lacking, it seemed, the confidence to make the final contact. One is certainly imbued with a huge respect for these great mammals when one is in their enclosures and at the mercy of their moods, which fortunately are benign most of the time. Unlike the elephant, the rhino will not submit to any sort of discipline. Juvenile elephants have to respond to the manifold pressures of herd life. In captivity they can be compelled to accept the authority of their mahouts or keepers after a rigorous training period. Not so the black rhinoceros. In nature he answers to no one and his independent spirit cannot be broken. The ancient Egyptians used rhinoceroses for their religious processions, but I strongly suspect they were of the docile white species which can still be found as far north as the Sudan.

Black rhino are true solitaries and Schenkel and Goddard's studies give a strange insight into their weird lives. The popular conception that they are pea-brained, lumbering buffoons is totally dispelled. *Diceros bicornis* at the apex of the faunal scale, master of his surroundings and almost without enemies until the advent of firearms, enjoyed an enviable existence for millions of years and survived in considerable numbers well into the last century. Unlike the elephant he is a sedentary species and therefore is more vulnerable to droughts. If his water-holes dry up he dies. In the past this was no great problem, though no doubt a restrictive factor on his geographical range. For one thing, he was widely distributed from Sahelia to the Cape, wherever savannah or low-density bush was predominant, and for another he naturally made sure that permanent water was available. Man-induced droughts that have decimated his numbers recently, in areas like Tsavo, were fortunately unknown in pre-history. The lowering of the water-table by extraction for industrial and residential use are body blows to the black rhinoceros. His numbers are now believed to have fallen to below 10,000 and with the troubles now afflicting Angola, Mozambique and Rhodesia, who can say what the future holds for him, if anything? Perilous though his predicament undoubtedly is, he is better off by far than his Asiatic cousins the Indian, Javan and Sumatran rhinoceroses. These three put together number not much above a thousand, spread from Nepal to Java. In Kaziranga in Assam and Chitwan in Nepal, the great Indian rhinoceros has its last redoubts where it is still protected, and in northern Java at Ulan Kuyong, the kindred Javan race has found its last refuge. The Sumatran, a two-horned species with a long red coat, is the rarest and the smallest and most likely to go first, as nowhere is there a known viable breeding population. The Sumatran appears to be the most solitary of all and thanks to continuing persecution and habitat shrinkage, it is doubtful if enough of them will ever meet up with each other for the race to continue to reproduce effectively. No zoo in the world exhibits a Sumatran rhinoceros. The last one in captivity died some years ago in Copenhagen.

Elephants tend to resent domination as they grow into adulthood and in the case of bulls their intractability has become proverbial. Most zoos refuse to keep bull elephants. Even Sir Hugh Casson's huge new Elephant House in the London Zoo, donated by Sir Michael Sobell, has no accommodation for bulls. In the whole of Britain there are fewer than a dozen bulls, and four of them are at Howletts. It is a scandalous fact that a successful birth has never been recorded in Britain (though a dead foetus was delivered at Chester Zoo in 1974), even though hundreds have been imported for 'exhibition' purposes since the arrival of Jumbo a century ago. On a world scale, breeding groups are an extreme rarity. To my knowledge, only Hanover has bred both the African and Indian elephant, whilst Krönberg (African), Basle, Budapest and Aalborg (Indian) represent the other successes in Europe. In America, Portland Zoo, Oregon, is famous for its record with Indian elephants, having bred eleven over the years. One of the prerequisites of success is a good 'bull hand'. Ideally an elephant keeper must stay with his charges for life. Usually the adult bull will only respond to the keeper or keepers he has known all his life. When they go on 'musth', approximately twice a year, they can become uncontrollable and have to be chained on all four legs and starved to boot. The connection with 'musth' and the sexual urge is obscure and it can be extremely dangerous to let a bull have access to a cow in this state, particularly if the enclosure is a small one. Copulation will often take place outside the 'musth' period, and it is possible that the aggression that 'musth' inspires in the male may be instrumental in their establishing dominance over the cows. It seems that no mating is possible without the almost abject submission of the female, a submission that is induced by fear. This hypothesis is born out by Eisenberg's study of the breeding behaviour of wild Sri Lankan elephants.

At Howletts we have a group of six Indian elephants, two bulls and four cows. The eldest bull – Assam – was born on 14 February 1968. We know his age as his birth took place in Hanover and he was the only one in the group not taken from the wild. The rest were chosen at an elephant market in Bihar. They travelled by freighter from Calcutta and were in a sorry state on arrival at Howletts. Some still wear deep scars round the neck, the result of being trapped in a keddah or wooden stockade and then roped to a tame elephant for training. The Indian group has been with me for five years and the oldest, Ranee and Buria, are nearly nine years of age. They are unlikely to mate for six or seven years so we are still a long way from breeding an elephant, but at least we are laying down the conditions to make this possible. The African group of two bulls and two cows are on a similar time scale. They are all approximately five years old and we hope to report a birth in the early 1980s. By then both species will be well on the way to extinction in the wild. The Indian elephant will bow out first as his preferred habitat, montane, broad-leafed forest, is now approaching relict status. The Indian forestry department admits to only seven per cent jungle area remaining. There are still a few herds on the *terai*, in the Orissan flat-jungle and in the high range of the southern Deccan. How long they will be allowed to live there is anybody's guess, but attempts at forest protection by the Indian government have faltered in the face of the voracious demand for hardwoods by six hundred million Indians. On my last trip to Corbett National Park in northern India I was horrified by the continual relays of trucks loaded with the precious *sal* wood, all of it lumbered from the Himalayan foothills inside and outside the park. I saw wild elephant at Corbett and a driven tiger which my wife Sally managed to photograph from a machan, the only tiger I have ever seen in the wild state. Though the culture of training elephants is thousands of years old in India, the animal is not really a domestic species as no consistent breeding has ever been accomplished in captivity. The elephants are wild-caught and so have not suffered the process of guided selective breeding that has altered the appearance of so many domestic animals almost out of recognition. Elephants are trained as beasts of burden,

Sally with Buria and, in the background, Pugli

for teak extraction and for processional purposes. Their lengthy gestation period, twenty months for a heifer calf and twenty-two for a bull calf, and the prolonged lactation that lasts several years, made attempts to breed highly uncommercial, as the cow would be unfit for work for so long.

The cost of maintaining ten elephants increases as their appetites enlarge with age. At the moment they account for fifteen bales of special home-grown hay a day, plus, depending on the season, one-and-a-half tons of mangold wurzels, maize or marrow-stem kale. Other favourites are brewer's grain, of which they get two tons a week during the winter, radish tops, turnips, potatoes and feed carrots. Though they will down large quantities of fresh grass, the summer season provides them with a variety of leaves and branches as well. Preference is shown for oak, sweet chestnut, horse chestnut, sycamore and thorn; ash and elder they won't touch. It is hoped at Port Lympne to give the elephants about six acres of grassland. They will be allowed on to this during the growing season when the ground is hard enough to prevent deterioration of the turf. We hope that, sometime in the early eighties, Assam will mount Ranee or Buria and become the founding dynast of a long line of Indian elephants.

It was no surprise to me to discover the upright, predictable and affectionate character of wolves. I had read Lois Crisler's *Arctic Wild* just before the arrival of Kago and Nushka from Whipsnade eleven years ago. The Crislers had reared abandoned Arctic wolves in the northern territories of Canada from puppyhood to maturity and had only good experiences to report of their foster children. Kago and Nushka were Canadian timber wolves and were about six weeks old when I first saw them. Though I have never cared much for dogs, wolves were a different proposition. There are over twenty epithets and expressions in the English language which refer to the wolf – all of them derogatory or pejorative in implication. Our hatred for this animal must stem from the recent pastoral epoch when the great northern forests were rapidly felled and replaced by grassland for cattle and sheep. During the severe winters the wolf, largely deprived of his natural prey – deer and wild boar – became a competitor of ours for beef and mutton. Man declared war on the wolf and in the process attempted a character assassination. It is only in the last twenty years that the true nature of this beautiful pack-hunter has become known; thanks to the work of Crisler, Mech, Farley Mowat and the revealing studies on Isle Royale, Lake Superior. After acquiring Kago and Nushka we added five more young wolves to the group and eagerly awaited the signs of mating behaviour. For four or five years nothing happened and it was the Isle Royale papers that gave us the clue. Kago and Nushka were the leaders of the pack and

Nushka was born in Whipsnade and means 'Look Look!' in the Iroquois tongue. When one sees her one cannot help but look long at her, for even among wolves she must be a great beauty. Nushka is a Canadian timber wolf and her ancestors came from the vast North West Territories, the land of the muskeg and permafrost, the land of the caribou

106

only they, we discovered, were allowed to breed. For some reason they had never done so but had effectively prevented any attempts by other members of the pack. We separated them into two groups and next spring six puppies were born to Yahooks and Onje, the leaders of the second group. They have bred regularly ever since. This restriction on breeding is a classic example of nature's behavioural wisdom. It not only ensures population control, but determines that the most adaptive genes survive. In the case of homo, the opposite is the case. The least successful breed the most, encouraging what Sir Julian Huxley called the 'survival of the sickest'.

I have never had a bad moment with my wolves, though I only have an intimate relationship with four or five animals. When I enter their enclosure as I do two or three times a week, I look upon them as my wolf pack as indeed I am part of it. Kago, Nushka, Tassialuk, Sahoni, Onhape, will all mill around me with an undisguised welcome. When I howl they follow suit, and if I fail to howl they will give tongue ten minutes after I have left. Once a she-wolf escaped into the countryside when I was staying in Normandy. I rushed back to Howletts when I got the news and was horrified to hear that the local newspapers had set up a hue and cry that had succeeded in terrifying many of the local villagers. The escaped wolf was called Little Bear and she was by no means the friendliest of the pack. She had been located in an orchard three or four miles away. I arrived at night, armed with a dead chicken, and howled into the wind. She answered me and a few minutes later I shoved her and the chicken into the back of the Land-Rover. She had eaten nothing for five days and had not attacked a sheep or a fowl. The headline of the local newspaper ran 'Escaped Wolf Terrorises Local Villages'.

Though unprovoked attacks on humans are virtually unknown as far as the Canadian timber wolf is concerned, I have little doubt that the sweet smell of sweating horse-flesh must have proved irresistible to winter-starved European wolves in the remote past. Wolves emboldened by hunger must have accounted for a few isolated wood-cutters and charcoal burners, but I cannot see why such behaviour should incur so much resentment. The likelihood of the Red Riding-Hood legend is that the grandmother ate the wolf and used its skin as a bed rug. Northern European man in the pre-pastoral epoch had a great admiration for his fellow pack-hunter. The ancient pagan Germanic names suggest this, Wulfhere, Wulfstan, Ethelwulf, Beowulf, Wolfgang and numerous others. Was not the wolf the friend of Odin? Even the early Romans revered the wolf. Romulus and Remus would be turning in their graves on the Janiculum if they knew what was happening to the last few wolves in Italy today.

Apart from the two races of tiger, we keep half a dozen other types of wild cat including black and spotted panthers, snow leopards, serval cats and northern lynx. The snow leopards are recent arrivals on loan from Lincoln Park and will be out of quarantine and into their new cage in 1976. We are building a forty-five feet high enclosure for them around a huge elm that has just died of the Dutch elm disease. Also recently arrived, from Frankfurt Zoo, are a pair of the rare Amur leopard – *Panthera pardus orientalis*. To secure this pair we have given in exchange a pair of clouded leopard and four Siberian tigresses. The snow and Amur leopards are among the most spectacularly beautiful and rare of the large cats and when they reach breeding age we have every hope they will reproduce their kind.

Among the hoofed stock at Howletts is the largest concentration of Indian species in Europe. Safari parks tend to exhibit the easily procured and easily replaced African animals. Grant's zebras, hybridised giraffe, common eland, East African baboon and the ubiquitous white rhinoceros. All these flung together with a few ostrich or brindled wildebeeste represent the audience-catching formula that can be seen in over a hundred drive-through safari parks throughout the west. The Indian deer and antelope have prospered well in the old park. Our five axis or spotted deer have swollen to over fifty-eight of which we have removed ten to Port Lympne to start another herd and a further six are on loan to English zoos. The sambar herd is the only one in the United Kingdom and has increased from three to twelve. Many of the fawns of these two beautiful types of deer are lost because they are dropped in the winter. At Chambord in France it was noted that a herd of axis deer bred season-ally after sixty years of hit and miss. The harsh policy of allowing the winter born to die pays off in the end as the herd becomes hardy and almost self-perpetuating. I say almost, because additional feeding in the winter for deer confined in a park is essential. The sambar, a distant relative of the red deer, has a better rate of fawn survival than the axis because the hinds usually give birth in the wind shelters and move their offspring from one shed to another, seldom leaving them in the open. Even hardier are the diminutive hog deer whose fawns are the size of a half-grown rabbit. Their numbers at Howletts have grown from five to thirteen in six years and soon we plan to split the group and form another at Port Lympne where there is much more land for expansion. The hog deer is so called from its habit of diving wild boar-like into heavy cover when alarmed. I have seen them do this at Kaziranga in Assam.

The nilghai and blackbuck antelope have proved more difficult to husband than the deer because both are creatures of the dry lands and they find the

Roan antelope calf, the first to be born in Britain

climate and conditions of Kent too wet and soft in winter months. Nilghai like best the harsh dry scrublands of central India and blackbuck, the great Indo-Gangetic flat-lands where their phenomenal speed was at a premium. Both are reduced to remnants in India today, though on some ranches in Texas large herds of these two antelope have been raised for 'sport'.

African antelope are represented by the closely related roan and sable. Both are renowned for their courage and determination. Even the lion hesitates before he attacks either of these. Many a great cat has been speared on their corrugated horns, carried by both sexes alike. Unfortunately generations of 'trophy' hunters have taken their toll of bulls with the largest horns and it seems that roan and sable seldom carry heads as noble as those found in Africa a century ago. Their calves born at Howletts are the first of their kind to be reared successfully in Britain.

The next few pages show some of the many animals at Howletts and Port Lympne and some of the people who look after them.

(above) *Zarka, at about eleven months, challenges Wawa the bison during one of his walks in the park*

(above) *Baringo (left) and Rukwa at four and three years respectively. They are now at Port Lympne and proper mating has been observed* (below) *Some of the Przewalski's Horse, now at Port Lympne. This rare species from Mongolia may be extinct in the wild*

(above left) *Bull Sable antelope* (above right) *The original group of five wild boar have grown to 50 in a few years* (below) *Kung, the first breeding male clouded leopard*

(above) *The first three-clouded leopards born in Britain—all female*
(below) *A few of the Axis hinds*

Richard Johnstone-Scott

Jimmy Shave

Nick Marx

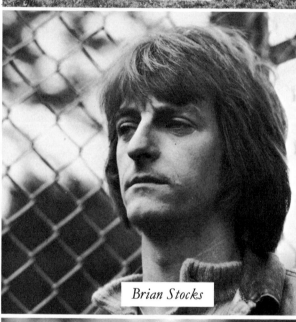

Brian Stocks

Paul Ottley

Peter Halliday

Sally, Koundu and Bassa

Lady Osborne

...es and Janie Osborne with Shuki and Yonkus

Tom Begg, the Howletts vet

(above) *Ugh, founding father of the bison herd*
(left) *Hog deer and fawn* (right) *Brazilian tapirs*

Narrow Escapes

I SUPPOSE that it is quite possible that I shall be killed by a wild animal. Sooner or later, with the passage of years, as the reflexes slacken and co-ordinative movements become more difficult, so the chances of an accident must increase.

In the autumn of 1959, I had my narrowest escape from death. It was my habit at the time to enter the large enclosure where I kept the two Himalayan bears, Esau and Ayesha. The animals were in their fourth year and were approaching adulthood. I had never had any real problems with them, though their play was so rough that I had double-thickness twill trousers made specially for their company and along with them, a heavy leather coat to protect me from their non-retractile claws. I had known the bears from infancy and had made a regular habit of jousting with them and joining in their games. One of their favourite activities was to suck my neck and to do this they had to climb up on me to reach it. If they attempted this simultaneously I usually collapsed under their weight. It was quite difficult then to extricate myself from their embrace once they had got going and I simply had to wait until they had had enough, which often took half an hour or more.

One afternoon, as was my wont, I decided to dress up and go and play with Esau and Ayesha. I took the precaution of putting on my cumbersome clothes and a heavy pair of ankle-length boots. When I arrived at their enclosure, which was surrounded by a ten-foot ha-ha ditch, I found that I had forgotten to bring the key. It was here that I made a grave error. I jumped into the pit – an easy task as the bank sloped away at an angle of forty-five degrees. I reckoned that I could shout to somebody when I wished to get out, as the area was adjacent to the main drive. Things immediately took a tricky turn. Esau was trying to copulate with Ayesha and she was not allowing him to mount properly. Each time he rose for a fresh effort, she rained blows on his head. I watched these proceedings from a distance of about thirty yards, not wanting, of course, to disturb them in any way. Esau finally looked at me after one of his abortive attempts and charged outright. I knew immediately that he meant business as he unleashed a series of frightful roars. The roar of an enraged bear is just as impressive as that of a lion, and has a nasal rather than a guttural tone. Esau fortunately was fat and unfit, whereas in those days I was in fair condition. There were three oak trees in the enclosure and I darted from one to the other in an attempt to exhaust him. I thought at first that his anger would abate in a few minutes, but this was far from the case. I was badly hampered by my heavy clothing but was reluctant to discard any of it as I thought it might prove to be some protection in the event of a clinch. However he got so close to me in one of his rushes that I hurled my coat at him hoping it would distract him. This ruse certainly gave me some respite, as he wasted several minutes tearing it to shreds. I did not view the spectacle with much relish, however, and having satisfied himself that there was no more life left in it, the bear once again hurled himself in my direction. With every outgoing breath I was now shouting for help, but no one was in sight or apparently in hearing. My stamina seemed to be ebbing, and then, unwittingly, Ayesha came to my aid. Esau ran past her, snorting and roaring and she turned on him thinking, no doubt, that she herself was the object of his aggression.

During this welcome interlude I decided to try and jump out of the enclosure. I took a twenty-yard run and jumped for all I was worth. I landed on the concrete wall with my elbows level with my shoulders. Under normal conditions I could easily have hauled myself out from this position, but sheer fatigue was my undoing. I slowly sank to the bottom of the ditch. In my despair I decided to lie low and hope that Esau had forgotten about me – out of sight, out of mind. I gathered a few large flint-stones and prepared myself for his arrival. A minute or so later he put in his appearance, weaving about above me, his eyes red with hatred. Luckily a bear likes to climb down a tree or a bank backwards. In an attack situation this puts him at a disadvantage and after one or two half-hearted attempts to lower himself down the bank, bottom first, he appeared to give up. I was no longer shouting, to conserve my energy for the final battle and also because I knew now that I was unlikely to be heard. After a puzzled look, Esau bundled off to the sloping path that led down to his sleeping den and adjoined the ditch. When I saw him coming towards me slowly and deliberately, I knew that he meant to settle the issue. I flung a rock at him and shouted his name with as commanding a tone as I could muster, hoping to revive in him some vestigial respect for his foster-father. He halted when the rock struck him, pained at my shouts, and then came steadily on. I remember at the time giving myself a twenty-to-one chance of survival. I was determined to die fighting, a crude flint in either hand.

In my mother-in-law's cottage meanwhile, she and a friend of mine called Richard Parkes had begun their tea. Dorothy Hastings had heard Esau's roaring and merely thought that he was involved in a fracas with Ayesha. They were so persistent, however, that she eventually went to the back door which was only 100 yards from the bear pit to try and determine what was afoot. She then heard my weakened cries and accompanied by the massive figure of Parkes, who weighed eighteen stone, and armed with saucepans and dustbin lids, they both converged on the scene of the battle. I heard them coming when Esau was about six feet from me. He pricked up his ears and fled, frightened by the sound and bustle.

They dragged me out and for an hour I sobbed while I clasped their hands. I could scarcely believe my good fortune. When it mattered, luck had been on my side.

From start to finish the whole incident probably only lasted about fifteen minutes, but to me it seemed an age. Why had Esau attacked me? The frustration of an unrequited love bound up, I suppose, with hierarchical ambitions. Either way, I never went in with him again as I thought that my ignominious flight would have convinced him of his superiority over me. I had lost face before him. Sadly, the bears never bred successfully and a few years later I sent them to Austria, as I needed their enclosure for a family of Siberian tigers.

At Christmas 1975 a most unusual and potentially dangerous event took place. Let Richard Johnstone-Scott tell it in his own words.

'At approximately 3.30 p.m. on Christmas Day I returned to the ape section to make up the evening feeds. I was greeted by the usual mixed chorus from both the chimps and gorillas in their anticipation of food. The excited screams of the chimps sounded strangely closer than usual and I walked round to the large exercise cage. There, I was confronted by the incredible sight of three gorillas and four chimpanzees thoroughly enjoying the novelty of being together in the same cage for the first time. I stood rooted to the spot for at least two minutes wondering if in fact I hadn't had too much wine with my lunch. Realising I was *not* seeing things, I climbed on to the catwalk and opened the slide leading to the smaller gorilla cages, at the same time calling to Shamba. She was sitting in the connecting tunnel coughing threats at any of the chimps who came too close to her, and was the only one of the four gorillas obviously not happy with the chimp invasion. Once the slide was open, she made a dignified exit, but Mumbah, Djoum and Mushie showed no intention of following her.

'I ran over the top of the big cage to the adjoining chimp enclosure, to discover the connecting slide was open and the padlock twisted into a corkscrew. I returned to the gorilla house, collected a spare padlock and an assortment of fruit and climbed back on to the cage roof.

'At this time, Djoum, Mushie, Jeni and Alexa were involved in a minor squabble of which Bongo seemed to be the cause. Jeni and Alexa were uttering short sharp hoots at Djoum who, with head down and arms waving, blundered his way between them, then ran off with them in hot pursuit. Mushie and Bongo joined the chase on the second lap of the cage.

'Meanwhile, Bustah and Mumbah were hammering up and down the metal shute, each seeming intent on deafening the other, and at the same time drowning out my pleas to the chimps to return to their cage. Bustah then set off across the floor of the cage with Mumbah at his heels, actually catching hold of his feet momentarily, a sort of tag game. Bustah eventually turned the tables on Mumbah and chased him back to the other side, both of them galloping on all fours at full stretch.

'By throwing a few apples, I succeeded in attracting Bustah's attention and he swung effortlessly up to greet me with a silly frantic grimace on his face. I tried coaxing him back into his own cage, but the temptation of the big cage and the gorillas was too much for him. He slid down a rope and rejoined Mumbah who was munching at a fist-full of apples.

'Bongo and Mushie, who had paired off from the others, took refuge in the chimp cage and ate a few titbits I had dropped in there. They were joined by Djoum, but once the food had been consumed they all returned to the big cage.

'At this stage Peter arrived, and by his looks and exclamations was as astounded as I had been on discovering this mixed group of ecstatic apes. For a few minutes we watched the gambolling, backslapping and brachiating (Mumbah swinging twice to every one of Bustah's), and then began a joint effort to separate the chimps from the gorillas.

'By now, Bustah's and Mumbah's groups must have been running together for about two hours, if not longer, but still the games continued. Bongo and Alexa began to show an interest in the pieces of apple and banana we scattered into the chimp cage and eventually they returned through the slide with Mushie close behind, but we managed to shut her out in time – causing her to scream hysterically.

'Bustah, Mumbah, Djoum and Jeni were now engaged in aerial follow-my-leader, crawling around on top of the brachiating bars with Bustah in the lead followed by Djoum, Jeni and the slightly less agile Mumbah. Seeing Bongo and Alexa eating in the chimp cage enticed Jeni and Bustah over to the slide to join Mushie. The slide was pulled open, but Bustah immediately swung away, returning to his game with Mumbah and Djoum. Jeni made it clear that she was in great need of food, but was not happy about eating it in her own cage. When a bar of chocolate was produced, her stubbornness wavered, and she reluctantly joined Alexa and Bongo.

'It was now quite dark and Peter and I were becoming desperate, but Bustah still romped with Djoum and Mumbah, while Mushie, feeling pangs of hunger, clung whimpering to the wire mesh below my feet. We succeeded in shutting Jeni, Alexa and Bongo in their bedroom and re-opened the connecting slide. After a certain amount of bribing with chocolate and bananas, Bustah moved across and sat by the opening, grinning at us. Seconds later, Djoum climbed up and joined him. Once again, Bustah lost interest and brachiated to the far end of the cage with the two male gorillas following clumsily, and this soon developed into another game of aerial tag. Mumbah dropped out and crossed over to the metal shute, impressing his weight upon it and producing an ear-splitting tattoo. Bustah, liking what he heard, swung down and joined in with gusto.

'Eventually, we decided to resort to using water as a persuader. Emptying the remainder of the bribes into the chimp cage, we pursued Bustah around the enclosure. Twice he passed the opening, treating this new chase as yet another game. Mumbah, thoroughly enjoying himself, followed, rumbling with excitement. We kept splashing water about a yard behind Bustah trying, at the same time, to keep an eye on Djoum and Mushie. With both Peter and I sweating heavily and facing defeat, Bustah suddenly decided to leave his gorilla companions, and enjoy the luxurious feed we had provided in the chimp enclosure. The slide was slammed shut and Mumbah, Djoum and Mushie were left staring enviously at Bustah wolfing down chocolate, bananas and biscuits. The chimps and gorillas had been together for most of the afternoon, and only once in all that time had there been any sign of aggression, and that had been the minor squabble, when Djoum had roughed up Bongo and been verbally reprimanded by Alexa and Jeni. Shamba had chosen not to mix with the group, but had treated the whole incident as fairly harmless and did not follow up her threats to the chimps.'

THOUGH I tend to write in a serious vein about animals, and though the purple patchwork of my prose may confound more than it persuades, I am bound to admit that the slow emergence in a placid valley in Kent of a fully-fledged zoo has given rise to some inherently comic situations.

The record of escapes is no worse at Howletts than in any other zoo of its size, but some of these have been accompanied by unwelcome splashes of publicity. On one occasion a keeper, whom I had sacked for negligence, let the pair of Himalayan bears loose. The last thing he did before he packed his bags was to open the padlock and unlatch the bolt of their sleeping den. It was during the apple-picking season and my neighbour, a prosperous fruit grower, had his work force in the orchards picking and crating. One of these men, from the vantage point of a tree, spied two bears loose in my walled garden and gave a shriek of alarm. Within minutes the orchard was deserted and the farmer was on his way to the nearest sitting judge in Hampshire, ninety miles away, to get a court order for the execution of the offending animals. Luckily for the bears, the judge did not comply as they had never left my land and so, legally, had not escaped. In the meantime they had a wonderful time in the vegetable garden rampaging around and flattening rows of carefully tended plants. Ayesha, the female, caused no trouble but Esau, her mate, terrorised the neighbourhood by uttering nasal roars and chasing everybody away who had the courage to approach him. We eventually lured them both into an empty chimpanzee cage with a bucket of green chartreuse. I had sent to the local pub for half-a-dozen bottles of this liqueur as it is famed for its sweetness and its strength – 120° proof. The two bears glugged down the thick green liquid and within half an hour both were drowsy. At this point I summoned two gardeners and a woodman and rolled Esau on to an improvised stretcher. The four of us carried him back to his den and dumped him in the straw without incident. With Ayesha, however, this method was less successful because the liqueur had all been in one bucket and Esau had hogged most of it. Ayesha's share was enough to make her sleepy but not enough to put her out completely. The result was that every ten yards or so she groaned or lurched or thrashed about on the stretcher. At the slightest movement from her the three helpers made for the greenhouse and left her heaving about on the gravel path. Finally, I poured enough brandy down her to put her into a deep sleep. The gardeners were reluctantly recruited, yet again, to give a helping hand and finally Ayesha was dumped next to Esau. The following day only deep snores and groans could be heard from their den and when after three days they did emerge, they looked like two bears with sore heads.

An earlier Christmas saw a most embarrassing escape. The gorilla keeper must have been suffering from the after-effects of a late night on Christmas Eve, because before he knocked off for lunch he clean forgot to lock the gorilla quarters. The result was that Gugis, then aged nine, and Shamba, aged ten, each weighing approximately 200 pounds, decided to take a walk. As they ambled round the garden, delicious smells came their way from the direction of some farm cottages. The weather was cold and the apes were hungry. Undeterred by the weather or the strangeness of the terrain, they decided to investigate. They climbed the garden wall and headed for the first cottage where a large family was about to sit down to the heaviest lunch of the year. The table was laden with Christmas pudding, crystalised fruits, dates and mince pies. The family of farm-workers were about to say grace when the door-handle turned and two gorillas walked into the room. The apes had, probably, never even in the vividness of their dreams, seen so sumptuous a repast. The table groaned with delicacies of which they were inordinately fond. Doubtless they thought that all had been carefully assembled for their delight, anyway a few minutes later they reappeared in my garden festooned in luxuries of which, in the normal course of events they would have been lucky to receive a nibble. They were so overloaded that they had adopted the bipedal walk. That was when I first saw them from my mother-in-law's cottage window, and I knew at once what had transpired. Gugis and Shamba were only too pleased to repair to their dwelling so that they could enjoy their loot at leisure, and after locking them in, I paid a visit to the scene of the debacle. The Christmas lunch was a wreck. The children of the family were crying quietly, it seemed more from fear than deprivation. I apologised lamely for the behaviour of my gorillas and offered to reimburse them ten-fold for the stolen groceries. As it happens, they were never mollified. To lay waste a Christmas lunch is an unpardonable crime in England. Even today, twelve years later, they pass me by in silence averting their eyes from my remorseful gaze.

On another occasion, two workmen arrived to wallpaper some bedrooms at my mother-in-law's cottage. To them, in the heat of a summer afternoon, this was just another run-of-the-mill job. On arrival they failed to take notice of the signs that indicated the presence of wild animals. In those days there were few enough of these, as we were not open to the public. When they appeared at the back door Mrs Hastings, who was expecting them, told them to mount the stairs and start work. 'The magnolia pattern is for the bedroom on the left of the stairs,' she said, 'and the morning-glory vine pattern for the room on the right.' 'Very good, ma'am', came the answer as they gathered in hand their buckets of glue and rolls of paper. As they began to climb the stairs noisily with their heavy boots, Mrs Hastings admonished, 'Don't make too much noise, there are two gorillas asleep up there. They like their sleep as much as you do' – a lengthy pause followed and one of them said, 'Blimey, she's a nut'. The wallpaperers started work without bothering to check for the presence of any gorillas. In the course of their trade, no doubt, they came across many eccentric old ladies and thought nothing more of it. Unfortunately one of them took it upon himself to whistle a melody and the high-pitched notes disturbed the two gorillas asleep together at the bottom of the bed. Mouila and Baby Doll had completely covered themselves with blankets and the workmen merely saw the bed heaving. When two black heads appeared and yawned simultaneously, displaying huge sets of canines, they downed tools and fled. In their frantic attempt to escape, they knocked over the glue bucket and startled the neighbourhood with their strange cries. They were never seen again.

The diving tiger, Zemo, was brought up in the house until he was nearly two years old. At that age, a tiger has put on sixty-five per cent of his growth. We let Zemo wander at will round the house and garden and on the whole he caused us very little trouble. It was all too good to last however, as one morning a lorry arrived with twenty hundredweight-sacks of coke to deliver. The driver was new to the area and ill-prepared for the events that followed. He unloaded the sacks in the stable yard and, having ascertained from the butler which cellar they were to be dumped in, started to carry them one at a time down the tunnel to the basement. Now Zemo was having his siesta in a laurel bush and took notice of the number of sacks which seemed to be disappearing into the bowels of the house. His favourite game of all was pouncing on a sack and tearing it to shreds, pretending it was his prey. He was normally rationed to about two sacks a week and could scarcely believe his eyes as the coalman passed him again and again, sack on shoulder. Zemo stalked him, after the fashion of his kind, his presence entirely unsuspected. The man, having completed half his task and emptied ten sacks in the cellar, decided to take a breather and light a cigarette. He sat himself on top of the sacks and struck a match. What the glare of the match revealed is probably still imprinted on his memory. It was the face of a tiger, a tiger about to spring. He screamed in terror, being convinced, no doubt, that he was about to face a terrible though unexpected death. The yell aroused Zemo to a pitch of excitement. He leapt ten feet at the sacks, brushing the paralysed coalman aside, and with a burst of savage growling proceeded to tear them to pieces. When my butler arrived on the scene to investigate the uproar, he found the poor man on his knees blubbing out the Lord's Prayer. He was so shaken that even the intake of two large brandies was insufficient to steady his nerves enough to enable him to drive back to the yard. We put him in a taxi and someone else was sent to collect his lorry next day.

A curious incident took place in the summer of 1965. Some friends of mine who lived near by, Michael and Anne Tree, were in the habit of coming over for lunch several times a year and then joining the gorillas for an afternoon stroll in the park. One Sunday, Michael called up and asked if he could bring his houseparty over. I agreed, of course, and was mildly surprised to see Lady Diana Cooper alight from one of the cars. She appeared to me to be somewhat frail for a gorilla ramble. I remember taking Michael Tree, and Michael Astor, who was also among the group, aside and making my fears known. Astor was duly apprehensive, but the others were made of sterner stuff. I was sufficiently impressed by this, but thought it wise to warn her that the cloche-shaped hat she was wearing would prove irresistible to one of the apes, Mouila, who was a compulsive hat-thief. To my astonishment she refused to part with it. I elaborated, pointing out that the shape of her headpiece was such that a sudden wrench on it might break her neck. 'I can't believe' she answered, 'that these delightful gorillas we have just seen have not the most perfect manners.'

Before we started on the walk I ordered the keeper to shadow Lady Diana and ensure that Mouila had no opportunity to get near her. The inevitable happened. While our attention was elsewhere, Mouila stole upon Lady Diana from behind, grabbed her hat and in the process of securing it, threw her violently to the ground. We all thought it was the end, as for a moment she lay still in the grass. Her neck, so swan-like in its youth, had retained its fragility. How could it have failed to have snapped? Diana provided us with the answer by rising to her feet with extraordinary dignity, the famous face almost hidden, Medusa-like, by a hundred clattering curlers. Far from being embarrassed by this exposure of her reasons for keeping her hat on, she continued the walk as if nothing had happened. The hat was recovered (somewhat the worse for wear) after a lengthy chase, and restored deftly to its original position. She had survived the whole ordeal unscathed.

Epilogue

Epilogue

MANY pressures have built up within me in the past decade, and these have now burst forth in the form of arduous and painful longhand. These forces are the work of guilt and shame: guilt at the tasks I have left undone – those of persuasion and conversion – and shame in the knowledge that I have in no small degree the abilities to undertake these tasks, yet have so rarely used them. This book, such as it is, is an attempt to redress the balance. The opinions and philosophy that will be expressed in the following pages represent the views of a vocal minority within the wildlife movement. We are the vanguard of the 'wild-politik'. The bulk of nature-lovers look upon us with bewilderment, not unmixed with hope. The great urban biomass gazes past us without comprehension, for we represent something which it has never understood and probably never will – the justice, the beauty and the relevance of the natural world.

This particular book is mostly about the high mammals, our 'next of kin' as Henry Salt called them. Certain of these, the tiger, the lowland gorilla, the timber wolf and the black rhinoceros, tend to dominate the pages. This is because the book is a subjective one. The animals portrayed are mostly my personal friends, and many of them were born at Howletts. The Zoo Park has grown organically from the smallest beginnings, and the profound relationships that have been established between myself and the keepers on one hand and the animals on the other have been the work of eighteen years. We feel at Howletts that we have pioneered this field in a manner heretofore untried, and

to some degree been successful in bridging that great man-made divide that has separated us from our kindred for countless thousands of years. To cross this bridge and enter the unknown land is a sensation not given to many. To enter the world of the tiger as a tiger; to join the wolf pack as a wolf; to be accepted as a member of a gorilla band and to live with them as they grow to maturity: these are some of the experiences which have become the daily routine at Howletts. As our respect for the mammals has steadily grown, so our excitement has never faded. To be admitted into their confidence and partake of their affection is a privilege which is not lost upon us. Many have feasted with kings, few with tigers. To those who say how dull must be the company of creatures that have no language or learning, I would answer that the most profound communications are often mute, and that we can learn more from the great mammals than we can possibly teach them.

Tameness is an inadequate term to describe the goal at which we strive, which is a mutual transfer of trust and affection between man and beast. To tame, according to the Oxford English Dictionary, is to 'subdue, subjugate, curb, render tractable or docile' – hardly an appropriate description of the confident friendships that have evolved at Howletts, where the fear-reward system of animal training is despised. The only domination exercised is surrogate parental authority with young animals and its residue when they reach adulthood. Useful also is a capacity to sustain a high ranking in the case of social animals like gorillas, elephants or wolves. With animals of a solitary nature, like tigers or black rhinos, it also pays to keep up such a show of confidence as would be the hallmark of a powerful male. In the event, of course, of running into a challenge from a full grown male tiger or rhinoceros, both of which have happened to me on occasions, a dignified retreat is the only recourse. Unarmed man, however strong, is quite powerless against even an adolescent tiger. To know them, to play with them, to love them, to share their company, is a lesson in humility, personal and specific. Personal in the obvious physical sense of being powerless in their presence, yet uplifted and honoured by their attention, and specific because nothing is so humbling to our species as to know and realise what we have done with the dictatorial power that we have come to possess over creatures that are manifestly superior to ourselves in so many ways.

According to Ericson and Wollin in their book *The Deep and the Past*, man's accession was a genetic fluke, 'an accident, the culmination of a series of highly improbable coincidences'. The professor adds that if man had not been a 'wrangling libidinous scoundrel he would never have made his way to his present evolutionary pinnacle'. Absolute power has corrupted absolutely. It seems that this power has been acquired by a species incapable of wielding it with justice and generosity. Plutarch writes of 'Nature's magnanimity', Churchill advised 'in victory magnanimity', but in actuality dominant man has been the greatest curse the planet has ever known. Edward Gibbon tells us that 'Attila the Hun, the Scourge of God, such was his ferocious pride, boasted that no grass ever grew where his horse had stood'. Mankind has made good Attila's idle vaunt, and even if a pandemic destroyed our whole species within a decade, the earth would bear the scars of the human experience for tens of millions of years, and even then could never recover the 'lost genes' that have fallen to our hand. Time can only heal some wounds. It cannot expiate the crimes of speciocide. The lengthy and forlorn dossier of our misdeeds invites remorse; remorse for the irremediable, for that which cannot be undone and which cannot be atoned. Out of our misery some of us can swear with Hannibal-like fervour to save what can be saved, to protect the wild places: others to breed what can be bred and tirelessly to incite the few that have the capacity to care. It is incumbent upon the faithful to understand that the whole tempo of the argument must be raised to a pitch of alarm to suit the hour. Moderation has demonstrably failed. The middle path must be abandoned. We must remember the old saw 'of the three roads to hell it is the middle one that is flattened by the feet of men'. To adapt Senator Goldwater's dictum 'extremism in defence of the biosphere is no crime'. Emotion is the philosopher's stone that will turn the base metal of apathy into the gold of action. Was it Democritus who said that 'Emotion is the Father of Action'? All I know is that without it the battle is lost. When I speak to an audience I must reach their pity. Hobbes said that 'grief for the calamity of another is pity'. Anglo-Saxons hide their emotion beneath layer upon layer of inhibitions which must be torn aside to reveal the auriferous rocks of their compassion.

George Schaller has written that 'those who know the most fear the most'. The pessimism of those who work in the field is reinforced by the compilers of statistics in London and Washington. Wild nature is visibly shrinking. As the technosphere expands the biosphere retracts. Man has forgotten that we owe everything to nature. The totality of our debt is manifest, our willingness to pay anything back on account barely discernible. Our only solution is to steal more and more of her dwindling resources and feed them into the industrial boiler, while hoping that it will blow up in the next generation, rather than in our own. Some of us are now driven to believe that a demo-catastrophe will be an eco-bonanza. In other words, a population readjustment

on a planetary scale from 4,000 million to something in the nature of 200 million would be the only possible solution for the survival of our own species and of the eco-system or systems that nurtured us. The reduced figure would represent a human population approximately equivalent to that of Julius Caesar's time, and may be too large for the earth to sustain in perpetuity. The Black Death halved the population of Eurasia within a few years. The next great death might last a millenium, but during it, and indeed before it, who knows how many genera of plant and bird and beast would be swept away? The followers of Gautama Buddha, the Judeo-Christians, the disciples of Mohammed and Marx can all look forward to some distant chiliad, but not the earth-lovers. The question that faces them is eschatological. What will be left? What will survive the holocaust? The surviving world must be a diminished world: at its worst, a world in apocalyptic, irreversible decline; at its best, one savagely mutilated, even dismembered. Many are tempted to ask whether there is any effective course of action. The truth is that man acts largely on basic impulse and is seldom prompted by reason, so his character is sculpted by genetic determination rather than environmental pressures. We act because we must: the paradox is that those who 'know the most and fear the most, act the most'. Humans like all other animals are constricted by their own nature and trapped within the confines of their own abilities; as Schopenhauer says, 'It is a wise man who knows his own limitations'. It is one of the saving graces of the human spirit that it can blind itself to unwelcome truths. Wildlife workers can be compared to the Sondergruppen of Auschwitz who actually knew the day they and their wards were to be executed and yet went on with their tasks as if there was no tomorrow. S.S. camp officials picked the Sondergruppen for their physical condition, but wildlife workers are ordained by the vagaries of the genetic mix. I suppose they have a greater empathetic reach than other men and are less prone to the besetting sin of hubris. The average citizen firmly believes in his own godhead and willingly swallows the sweet pabulum prepared for him by his religio-cultural chefs. The human race can be likened to the hero of a Sophoclean tragedy, brave, gifted, fortunate, but susceptible to an inane pride that turns to hubris. The peripeteia, the point of no return, is reached when he deems himself a god. From then on the tragedy unfolds and reaches its climacteric in death. The hero is destroyed by an overweening pride that has curdled into madness. The author knows it. The audience has sensed it. Only he himself is unaware of the fate lined up for him. That shop-worn cliche 'The sanctity of human life' sums it up in a phrase. This concept is probably the most damaging sophistry ever propagated. It has rooted well.

The cause of the damage is clearly seen when we examine its implicit corollary 'the insanctity of life other than human'. Edward Goldsmith in his essay 'Religion in a Stable Society' confirms unequivocally that by 'desanctifying our environment it has become possible for modern society to systematically destroy itself'. No amount of tears can wash away this most welcome of all received ideas. Timur with his mountain of hands, Shaka's singing impis, Hitler with his 'final solution', the massacred millions of Stalin and Mao Tse-tung – all these have failed to dislodge the evil djinn from our shoulder.

The grand design of all wildlife workers must be to protect the threatened through this difficult time. To conserve wilderness and save species is their overriding aim. Evolution, it is estimated, discards one species of animal every thousand years. Mankind exterminates one species each year, so usurping the ultimate prerogative of deciding which shall exist and which shall not exist, and even accelerates the process a thousand fold. We seem to be singularly ill equipped to bear so august a burden. Any cursory study of history or pre-history would soon sweep away any illusions on that point. Power has fallen into the hands of a *parvenu*, a pinchbeck overlord who rules to satisfy what he sees to be his short term need at the expense of the rest of creation. To enable him to go ahead with this war of attrition without qualm of conscience he has raised himself into a godhead – a convenient myth which is endorsed by all the great religions except Buddhism, which itself is in terminal decline possibly because of this rejection and has degenerated into liturgical sacerdotalism. Anthropocentrism is the common factor of Islam, Judeo-Christianity and Marxism, a troika only designed to carry one passenger, man himself in the image of God, *homo imago dei*. Marxism is the direct heir of Christianity in this respect and is unfortunately much more effective in ramming its lessons home. The indigenous nations of the non-industrial world have forsaken their animistic ancestor-worship for the new heresies. Their old tribal beliefs, circumscribed as they were by countless behavioural wisdoms, inhibitions and taboos, have been destroyed at enormous cost in population increase, habitat destruction and loss of identity. The old restraints have been eroded. Negative wisdom, the work of tens of thousands of years of experience, has been replaced by positive knowledge. The end result will be unimaginable catastrophes. The only things more dangerous than knowledge is more knowledge.

The terrible truth is that our species is incompetent, ham-handed and arrogant to boot. We are intelligent, it is true, possibly the most intelligent of all the species, though the whales and the dolphins must run us close, but what use is intelligence unallied to wisdom? Seneca said that 'no amount of intelligence

can add up to wisdom'. We have ingenuity, but what use is ingenuity if it is counter-adaptive or over-adaptive? 'Adapt or die' runs the old adage, but over-adapt and you invite over-death. Along with intelligence and ingenuity we have cunning, that 'dark sanctuary of incapacity' as Chesterfield described it. To top it all we, as a species, have a surfeit of energy. It is energy that has acted as the ruinous catalyst; that has prised open Pandora's Box and used its contents as missiles to destroy a planet. Nature provides that the most powerful of her species are the most inactive or the most gentle. The great cats sleep seventeen hours out of twenty-four and kill infrequently, once every five or six days, when driven by the hunger urge. Confident of their power, they seldom use it. Before the advent of the *parvenu* they sat at the apex of the faunal pyramid, secure in their imperium. Good-natured, majestic, stable, they adorned the landscape and added to the system which had honoured them. The great gorilla, man's elder brother, combines Cyclopean strength with an unwillingness to hurl thunderbolts at Zeus. He is the possessor of those qualities that the ancients admired but found in such short supply, *Dignitas, Gravitas, Nobilitas.* He shared the great African rain forest with us in the Pliocene and is, indeed, a living proof of our own identity as a species – a companion of our past and, we hope, a talisman of our future. He is a relative on whose account we must feel pride and gratitude – pride in our kinship, and gratitude for the lessons of his example: how to dominate habitat without destroying it – how to maintain primacy without voracity.

The great overlords of nature seldom veered from the wide roles that they enjoyed. The sperm whale could roam the oceans without disturbing them. The American bison could wander at will over a grass sea the size of India and be numbered in tens of millions without injury to the endless swards that in fact they maintained. *Carcharodon carcharias*, the great white shark, so perfect a model that it has scarcely changed morphologically for thirty million years, has taken nothing from the oceans that it has not returned after so long a dominion. It is a strange irony that these great hegemons can no longer protect themselves – that their destiny lies in our blooded hands. In our capacity to extend to them our love and understanding is their future measured. That this should be so is an evolutionary miscarriage, but that it is so is inescapable. Here sits *sapiens* on his imperial dais giving judgement like a Domitian or a Commodus in the Circus Maximus. He must raise his thumb to the expiring creatures beneath him in the sand. 'Hail Caesar! Those who are about to die curse you and those who are already dead condemn you, for in your paranoia you have sealed your own fate. The world you are mutilating is your world, your only possible world. The animals you have so eagerly destroyed are your own kindred, without whom you cannot live. Aeons will pass before your infamy will be forgotten and you will then join the bizarre group of evolutionary dead-enders along with the trilobites and ammonites.'

One of the compulsions that drives me to write is the pursuit of fame. Fame in the Nietzschean sense of the optimum use of abilities, the stretching to danger point of one's own gifts in heroic aspiration, with all the risks entailed and the enjoyment of those risks. Of one thing I am certain, and that is that if the history of my epoch is ever recorded by any species other than man then my efforts will not pass unnoticed. It is often said that people who love animals are misanthropes who have failed in their human relationships and have settled for a second best. This has not been my own experience, nor is it typical of animal lovers as a whole. I made my fortune by an ability to create and sustain a complex human connection, without which a gambler cannot survive for long. I would endorse Oscar Wilde's dictum that 'only shallow people cannot judge by appearances' and in the art of the gambler and animal lover, appearances count for a great deal. Misjudge them and the penalty can be expensive or even fatal. I find that my friends come to me with their deepest problems because they know that such problems often require a biological answer. In the same fashion, others will sometimes ask me as to the character of a person on a mere introduction. They listen to my response because the years have told them that my judgements, if I give them, have proved helpful. I like to think that wisdom and its derivative, judgement, seep from phylogenetic springs and have little concern with brilliancy or intellectuality, or, strange to say, experience. After all, everyone has experience, few have wisdom. In Schopenhauer's words, 'experience is only of phenomena, it is not knowledge of the thing in itself'. Look straight into wisdom's prism and you only see the baggage you have already hidden there, mostly, of course, the things that you want to see, but from a certain angle often stumbled on by mere chance and occasionally arrived at by long endeavour, the truth is revealed without refraction, in its purity. I attempt to unravel the verities from the standpoint of nature in the grand context of evolution. Though self-elect and self-appointed I feel that I am a spokesman, however inadequate, for wild things and I ask the reader to join me in this role. Let us be the eyes of the blinded, the voice of those whose tongues we have torn out, the ears of those whose drums have been dulled by our crescendo. Wild nature has no vote, no influence, no power, no hope even, unless we range ourselves, phalanx-like, at her side and cordon her last places. Her protection is the noblest and most necessary of all causes because it takes

138

man out of his own religio-cultural mælstrom and allows him to perform where he is needed most.

No longer can it be said that peace, plenty and plurality are worthy ends. The billions blown on medicare are monies ill-spent and worse than wasted. As Julian Huxley has it, *Homo sapiens* is in uncontrolled, cancerous growth and medical research has merely exacerbated this condition. Unfortunately its efforts to neutralise our time-honoured, natural beneficial predators like bubonic bacillus, the anopheles mosquito and the typhoid bacterium have proved only too successful. If an animal renders ineffective its own evolved cullers, then it has signed its own death warrant. Remove natural selection and the genes run amok. An irreversible process of genetic drift steals upon the species and guides it to the shambles. Eugene Marais, the pioneer ethologist, saw this fifty years ago, when he stated that any species that allowed deviants and aberrants to breed without restraint was doomed to extinction. Man is in the extreme condition of this laxity. Medical research should be funded into abortion, infanticide, euthanasia and birth control. Forms of unnatural eugenic selection should be studied, on the basis that unnatural selection is better than no selection. The question really is, whether we wish to save our species or not, for time is running out on us. The choice before us is a qualitative life for 200,000,000 humans in perpetuity in a partially restored paradise, or a quantitative countdown to Armageddon on a raped planet gutted of most of its resources. That we still have a choice or a chance may itself be an illusion. If one is dying of thirst in a desert even a mirage is welcome. Better to die stumbling forward lured by hallucinations than be wind-buried by the sands of despair.

I am sometimes asked as to the 'secrets' of gaining the confidence of beasts. In a sense there are two secrets; the first, respect, can be culturally acquired, the second, love, must be inborn. There is nothing more important than to respect the animals in your care. By this I mean that it is essential to feel that they are at least as important as the human race. If the concomitant of respect is love, then you have the beginnings of an animal man. All that needs to be added is patience, courage and some common sense.

Of course most people are ruled out on the score of respect. Nothing will ever convince them that other creatures are anything but deeply inferior to themselves. A high mammal soon discerns this attitude in a human, and resentment breeds aggression when he feels that he is merely an 'inmate', an object of curiosity or, to use the word so sadly popular with many zoos, an 'exhibit'. Just as a human knows whether he is a prisoner or a guest, so does a mammal. Respect is possibly the most important ingredient of all, and with many people love is a natural follow-up. Most high mammals, in my experience, are responsive to affection and return it in good measure. One must, however, love each creature after its own fashion. A tiger, for instance, is a mammal that craves for caresses and tactile communication and if the spirit takes him, likes these to be followed by horse-play. The first two present no problem, but romping with a tiger and participating in its favourite game, which is 'you're my prey', can be discomforting. This involves the tiger stalking you, preferably when your back is turned, pouncing on you, knocking you down and taking your neck between its teeth. Tigers also enjoy a boxing bout. For this procedure they rise on their hind legs, dancing in an ungainly fashion, and aim blows at your head or other parts of your anatomy. Both these pastimes would be insupportable if they failed to keep their claws sheathed.

Ernst Lang once told me that he talked to all his animals, and would not dream of passing by an old friend on his daily rounds without a greeting. This, which should come naturally to an animal-lover, is most important. A human can easily be put out of sorts if he is 'cut' by a friend: so can an animal. I find that my arrival elicits undisguised joy in many of the animals at Howletts, be they wolves, chimpanzees, gorillas or tigers. I find that my own reaction is similar. In the same way that my visit to them will enliven their day and enlarge their experience, so I myself feel restrengthened and replenished by contact. I have also encouraged the formation of emotional bonds between the keepers and their charges. How can I deny to them what has been my own particular joy? Most zoos do not encourage this relationship as it could be administratively inconvenient. To take a big-cat keeper and transfer him to camels would be asking for trouble if the keeper had grown to love his animals.

The danger of imprintation to the extent that it inhibits breeding is exaggerated, though hand-reared infants must be carefully reintegrated with their own kind after weaning. In the process of building a lasting relationship with a wild animal, one must remember that to effect this without mishap one must assimilate oneself as an honorary member of the species involved. On no account should one attempt to impregnate the wild animals with any human characteristics – to anthropomorphise – God forbid! The reality is that such is the impact of these relationships that the human himself is profoundly shaped and influenced by his experiences with animals. When I make love I gurgle like a gorilla; when in pain, I have been known to mew like a rhinoceros. On occasion I have even found myself unconsciously greeting friends with a tiger's welcoming purr – a noise peculiar to these big cats.

None of the animals at Howletts is 'worked' or taught any tricks, though we do attempt to give full rein to their natural proclivities as far as we can. Compared with the great urban zoological institutions and the Safari Parks, Howletts is grotesquely underfinanced. The total construction cost of all the animal installations at Howletts represents half the cost of London Zoo's Elephant House and one quarter of the estimated cost of the new cat house in that establishment – £690,000. What we have accomplished has been done without the weight of money. The London Zoo figures, impressive as they are, pale into insignificance when compared with expenditure in the New World. One of the five aviaries in the Bronx Zoo in New York cost over $4,000,000 and was endowed separately by the donors who are the proprietors of *The Reader's Digest*. At Brookfield Zoo, Chicago, Peter Crowcroft, its famous director, has $5,000,000 to deploy on a new Ape House which is now nearly complete. In San Diego, the Zoo has attendance money of $12,000,000 a year to dispose of, and maintains a faculty of over a hundred. The sum of our achievement has to be weighed against the size of our purse. Howletts – and Port Lympne – is one of the poorest zoos in the world, but rich in philosophical commitment, in dedication and in ambition.

Many great zoos are hamstrung by their ancient charters. Some like Lincoln Park, Chicago, and New York are compelled to admit the public free of charge. The consequence of this is to encourage the attendance *en masse* of the populace. The lowest social echelons usually have the greatest contempt for other organisms, and for places of entertainment that are provided free by the state or municipality. The concept that a zoo is for the people not the animals is perpetuated by the grave error of free admissions. Urban man respects what he pays for. Free handouts are taken but despised. It is astounding how some institutionalised establishments have managed to overcome their problems and set an example to others. Basle under Ernst Lang and Frankfurt under Bernard Grzimek have set the pace for Europe, while in the U.S.A. Bill Conway of the Bronx, New York, Les Fisher of Lincoln Park, Chicago, and Peter Crowcroft of Brookfield, Chicago, lead the field. The breeding successes of these five zoos are phenomenal. The five men who lead them can be favourably compared with their counterparts in the political and business world.

Bill Conway said to me once that he would like to see zoologists take over government. At least such an eventuality would herald the demise of anthropofascism. If I was given power in the United Kingdom, I would introduce a *Jus animalium* and a *Jus herbarum*, a bill of rights for animals and plants. From our earliest childhood we are all bombarded with the rights of man – the bill of

143

rights – the declaration of rights – civil rights – ethnic rights – women's rights – pupils' rights. Who has ever heard mention of the rights of beasts? Or the rights of birds and plants? Have they no rights also? If not, let us incorporate them into a new constitution, into a new religion. After all as the poet, De Vigny, says, animals are the 'rightful tenants of these woods and hills'. Have we no place for them – none to offer? Are we such strangers to justice that we cannot bring ourselves to give back to them a tithe of what was once their own? Are we such foreigners to pity that we cannot even mourn for them or drink from 'pity's long-unbroken urn'? The call goes forth from nature's advocates 'save them for our children's heritage', 'save them for one day their gene pools may prove useful to us', 'save them to enrich our cultural options'. I find these exhortations reek of hubris. What about their own heritage, their own gene pools proving useful to themselves? What about their own cultural or behavioural options? To have survived every geological catastrophe, every climatic change, every biological invasion, every genetic shift, every seismic upheaval since life emerged from the Cambrian slimes. To have accomplished all this, and even to have outlived what Professor Kurtèn, in *The Age of Mammals*, calls man's 'peripatetic pyromania', surely entitles them to be granted a stay of execution?

Kurtèn emphasises that 'if we persist in our futile war against nature our reign as a species will be brief indeed – shorter even than the Flandrian Interglacial!'. He adheres to the modern view that the discovery of fire approximately 750,000 years ago triggered the subsequent degradation of habitat. Until recently it was generally thought that the domestication of plants and animals and the resultant surplus economy was the initial cause of biotat decline. Frederick Zeuner in his *History of Domesticated Animals* hints at this but it seems clear now that civilization has merely compounded and accelerated an established process. The gods of Greece were not far off the mark when they punished Prometheus who 'stole' fire from Heaven by chaining him to a rock and having his liver torn out daily by eagles. By burning off vegetation over wide areas in order to drive game, early man destroyed his surroundings and caused far greater harm than that wrought by hunting alone. 'The presence of advanced human hunting cultures' adds Kurtèn, 'seems connected with a sudden decline of the large game. The correlation is so close that it is hard to escape the conclusion that the extinctions were caused in some way by the influence of man.'

As a species, then, we appear to have a crime sheet nearly a million years old. In Africa alone forty per cent of the genera of large mammals were destroyed –

giant baboons, sabre-toothed cats, three-toed horses and numerous other 'megafauna'. The surviving impoverished remnant is essentially the one in existence there today. At least the African species evolved alongside our ancestors through the Pleistocene and a fair number of them developed techniques of avoidance and resistance. When *homo* went on his Eurasiatic adventure and his ensuing intrusion into the New World the depredations that he made on the indigenous mammals were horrendous. In Eurasia the legendary mammoth (*Elephas primigenius*), the woolly rhinoceros, Merck's rhinoceros, the splendid cave bear (*Ursus spelaeus*), lions and cave hyænas, the giant fallow deer (*Cervus megaceros*) and countless others were butchered out of existence. Even this slaughter, protracted over about fifty thousand years, cannot bear comparison with the carnage inflicted on American animals by the early Mongoloid invaders. Some experts believe this mass death had a duration of one or two thousand years only – an episodic catastrophe that swept away the ground-sloths including the wondrous *Megatherium*, the giant beaver, the great prairie cat (*Panthera atrox*), the long-horned bison, the dire wolves, the mastodons, the imperial mammoths and tens of millions of camelids and wild horses. The climax ecosystem paid a heavy price for the presence of the Paleo-Indian hunters – a price only to be surpassed by hosting the Europeans – after what has been euphemistically called the Post-Columbian Intrusion.

Some thinkers believe that man alone has an evolutionary potential left, that all species that cannot be enslaved to his purpose are doomed. Professor J. H. Fremlin writing in the *New Scientist* in 1964 supports this view and proffers an ingenious theory that our numbers will increase exponentially until we reach the thermodynamic limit imposed by the dissipation of our metabolic heat (40 or 50 billion?). We will then live in groups imprisoned physically but free in the noosphere of Teilhard de Chardin, subsisting on a nutrient broth recycled from our own body wastes and permitted to produce one replacement infant per death. We and our synthetic yeasts or bacteria will then be the only inhabitants of spaceship Earth. Fremlin has worked out with some relish the details of how to operate this nightmare. Dr R. F. Ewer in her book *The Carnivores* ends on an unhappy note. Of course she rejects the Fremlin hypothesis, and hopes the human race can discipline itself to a policy of population reduction by voluntary means, but leans to the 'natural solution'. 'Most likely, she suggests, 'as we expand the natural disasters of disease and famine and mutual slaughter will decide our problems for us.' She regrets though that these readjustments 'will probably not occur until after we have destroyed much of our habitat and voided it of many of its potentialities'.

Man has been the spendthrift of his own genius and has seemed to take a curious joy in the misuse of his gifts. Nature knows of no more profligate hunter. He appears to be without the built-in restraints of fully evolved predators. This deficiency is age-old and age-proven. The character of man is to be found in the marl and breccia of a thousand caves. Among the sherds and detritus of the middens can the truths be unearthed. History is merely an amusing postscript to the aeons that preceded it. When Henry Ford described history as 'bunk' he stumbled on a profound truth. History has never repeated itself because it has never had time to do so – as Hegel said, the 'only thing we can learn from history is that history has nothing to teach us'. There is nothing more over-rated or more readable than history. What Arnold Toynbee said of history I would transpose to pre-history: he said 'History is not another subject, it is the house in which all other subjects dwell'. Toynbee's vision was constricted to ten thousand years – an inch in a mile-long race.

What history does seem to underscore is that the nature of man changes only imperceptibly in spite of rapid cultural aberrations or 'progress'. From Jesus to Marx, it has been the ambition of the reformer to create an 'ideal' behavioural mould from his own imagination, and then to pour the molten human bronze into it. Every time, the cast has broken the mould and, to the bewilderment of the 'bronzeur', set back into its original shape. It is a strange anomaly that at exactly that very moment today when post-Darwinian philosophers, drawing inspiration from recent ethological studies, have confirmed the soundness of time-held conservative tenets, the protagonists of the right have been subverted by their opponents. The Duke of Wellington believed it was the duty of an Englishman to resist all change. He saw the Tory party as the custodian of this political creed. As time passes so will his reputation for wisdom increase. Change, if it has to come, must be fought at every parapet, not encouraged to enter the citadel. If one is forced to submit to technological change, then in compensation one must resist social change. It is in social change and its sibling cultural change that the most danger lies. These three Furies have led us to the very gates of Hades.

Over a hundred years ago when Darwin asserted that we were related to the apes, the majority of the educated men of the time, including Wilberforce and Professor Owen, decried him. Today, when at our disposal we have the recent behavioural studies or ethograms of Carpenter, Schaller, Goodall, Reynolds, Kortlandt and others on various social primates, we have either ignored them or failed to draw from them the conclusions that lie embedded like gemstones in their work. If Pope averred that 'the proper study of mankind is man', then

the next best study of mankind is ape. Man is a social primate. Of the two hundred-odd species of high primate, all except the orang-utan and the gibbons are social. Certain factors and features are common to all social primates, including man: among them, linear hierarchy, male dominance, sexual dimorphism, and elitism. Benevolent patriarchates with gorillas – self-perpetuating oligarchies with Japanese macaques – hereditary royal families with Java monkeys – various dictatorships with gelada and hamadryas baboons; all these human social control systems are adumbrated in the simian world.

Even the studies of social primates in artificially dense, captive communities can be revealing. It appears that the more concentrated the numbers, the greater the tyranny. Zuckerman's pre-war study of hamadryas baboons in London Zoo gave the baboon tribe a bad reputation which it has now begun to live down. In the over-crowded enclosure where observation was made, violence, infanticide and other aberrations became commonplace and were aggravated by an inappropriate sex ratio. The main adaptive response to these artificially cramped conditions was the emergence of a despotic dictatorship. Though even in the wild state baboon troops tend to be autarchical in structure, they are without the unpleasant behavioural exaggerations observed by Zuckerman. Overcrowding is the father of violence. Bertrand Russell in his treatise on Bolshevism states that where human society is most urbanised there is the greatest social sickness. The irony here is that in a democracy where urban man outnumbers non-urban man we are ruled by those least fitted to rule – the socially sickest.

Dr P. Studer of Basle Zoo showed me a large troop of about fifty Java monkeys presided over by an hereditary royal family. He asked me, after I had studied this group for a few minutes, if I could pick out the alpha male. This was not difficult as one large, perfectly groomed monkey was clearly ascendant over all the others. Dr Studer informed me that this male had ruled the troop well and justly for several years but that his father, the previous dynast, had proved himself the proverbial 'bad king'. He said the whole tone and tenor of the Java monkey colony was dependent on the character and personality of the dominant male. The late king had been a mean, treacherous trouble-rouser and there were numerous cases of injuries and deaths during his reign. Now, however, all was well, there were few injuries, no deaths and much content-ment. I was astounded when he informed me that he already knew the likely heir-presumptive. Only the progeny of two or three high-ranking royal wives were eligible and of these there was one young male that elicited much more concern and attention from the females in the troop when he gave a cry of alarm or a screech of pain. In fact, the linear ranking of all the juveniles could be so determined. If a low-ranking female's infant screamed in alarm, only its mother comforted it. If, however, the 'heir' followed suit, all the females would cluster round and cherish him.

An ethogram of Java monkeys in the wild has confirmed the Basle findings. How long a single family can perpetuate its advantage is not known, but research on a close relation, the Japanese macaque, has lasted many years and bears out that privileged elites are not easily overthrown and may survive for generations. Japanese macaques have evolved a social system that features a small central ruling cadre, which enjoys whatever privileges and benefits are available to the band which can number up to five hundred members. The advantages which accrue to this elite are passed on to their progeny. 'Inequality of opportunity' is the primate slogan. The scions of high-ranking parents are probably the beneficiaries of genetic as well as cultural superiorities, and this suggests that aristocracy, in its literal sense of 'rule by the best', could well be the best of all rules.

Endless are the inferences that can be drawn and extrapolated from primate ethologies to the study of man himself – the arch-primate of them all. The human ape seems to have adopted many control-systems common to his cousins – on the whole, with considerable success. In vain have the 'Procrustean' reformers tried to stretch or lop their human victims to fit a bed designed on the best theoretical principles. Disaster inevitably follows, as the old primate behaviour patterns reassert themselves. A recent classic example of primate social pressures on a group of humans was evidenced by the conduct of the thirty-odd survivors of the Andean plane crash in 1973 when cannibalism was resorted to after ten days of near starvation. Piers Paul Read, in his excellent book *Alive – Survival in the Andes* gives a fascinating description of how the band of young Uruguayan Rugby players settled into a clearly-defined linear hierarchy. At the top arose a triumvirate of two brothers and a cousin, beneath them formed the *expeditionores* who thanks to their fitness and courage made a privileged warrior caste, after them came the craftsmen and artisans with their special skills, and last of all the misfits, cripples and no-hopers. Thanks to the guidance of the triumvirs, the hardihood and valour of the *expeditionores* and the patience and skill of the artisans the majority of the band survived. It is possible to glean more from a study of this 'documentary' about man's 'sociology' than from the toils of Marx, Russell and Marcuse. It should be compulsory reading for those who wish to understand the human animal, and for those who attempt to legislate for him.

Man's contempt for animals precludes him from accepting the validity of primate studies in relation to himself, and he shies at any inferences that can be drawn from them. Unfortunately nearly every human is subject to the relentless propaganda of language. It is with us from our earliest years and leaves an indelible weal on our psyche. The very words as we learn them conspire to defraud us of our judgement. Bestial, Beastly, Brutish, Brutal, can be compared to Humane, Manly, etc. There are hundreds of idioms in the English language which refer to animals. Nearly all of them are derogatory or pejorative in implication. To say that a man 'behaves like an animal' is to imply mindless violence, and is often used by judges when summing up in a criminal trial. The 'law of the jungle – red in tooth and claw' suggests shameless chaos and ferocity. The reality is very different. Mindless violence and shameless chaos are most in evidence among humans. I have spent many months in jungles and have always been impressed by the beauty and justice of the forest regimen. Violence if it does surface is mindful and infrequent, and chaos unknown – that is until man's incursion, when of course all is changed. 'Nature, whose sweet rains fall on just and unjust alike', has much to teach those who are willing to learn. But will they ever be enough to force a shift in opinion large enough to deflect the present collision course of our culture? I think not – I think the odds are stacked against success; but I know of no other wager worth a bet. Let us grasp the gamble with both hands and pray for time.

SOMEBODY once wrote about me that I would never make a success of my life or be able to use my talents to full effect as I always sought the thickest part of the battle where the risk was greatest and the reward the least. The writer added that I was circumscribed by my romanticism and weakened by my idleness. In a sense, all is true. If I had gone into politics my gift for persuasion, my oratorical powers, my capacity to incite admiration would have found an outlet that could have furnished me with influence and power far greater than the modicum that I now have at my disposal. But it could never have happened because my allegiance, my loyalty, my understanding, could never be at the beck and call of the suffrage. Whatever my faults, humbug and hypocrisy are not among them. Dissimulation, the soft-speak, the open elective bribery, the abasement before the demos and genuflexion before superiors, all are alien to my nature, my temperament, my view of myself. The jibe at my indolence has found a mark. If the gods had given me energy, I would have been a dangerous man. Single mindedness, a great rarity among humans, has always been in my possession, a confidence in myself, a sense of mission, even of destiny, shored up by a compelling evolutionary faith; all these are as nothing without the will and endurance that separate the gifted from the great. Like all men who realise at fifty that they have failed I seek compensation from posterity. In a thousand years or a million years will the road to Canterbury be thick with pilgrims come to weep at my shrine? Will they be human or non-human? Which would I want them to be? I am sure as a social primate I must seek responses from my own kind, posthumous or otherwise. Why else should I have written this book? These words are unlikely to be read by gorillas, dolphins or clouded leopards, and yet a premonition seizes me as I write that the understanding that I have will pass to many, will grip my heirs, wrench them from their lasts where they cobble their ruin in blindness. A whole earth is what I seek, nothing less than a whole earth – a whole security. Gambler that I have always been, brave man that I am, I tremble with fear before the oncoming storm. As the firmament darkens, as the thunder peals, let us stand side by side like our ancestors of yore, faces frozen by the wind, swords drawn for the last battle – the last great battle for the earth itself, the whole earth and nothing but the whole earth.

152

Credo

I BELIEVE a wildlifer must not expect to be rewarded with recognition or worldly approval. His work will be to him his recompense. Only in his own peace of mind and self-esteem will he find solace.

I believe in *Jus animalium*, The Rights of Beasts, and *Jus herbarum*, The Rights of Plants. The right to exist as they have always existed, to live and let live. I believe in the Buddhist concept of *Ahimsa* – justice for all animate things. I believe in the greatest happiness for the greatest number of species of fauna and flora that the Earth can sustain without resultant deterioration of habitat and depletion of natural resources.

I believe in the sanctity of the life systems, not in *the sanctity of human life alone*. The concept of sanctity of human life is the most damaging sophism that philosophy has ever propagated – it has rooted well. Its corollary – a belief in the insanctity of species other than man – is the cause of that damage. The destruction of this idea is a prerequisite for survival.

I believe that wilderness is Earth's greatest treasure. Wilderness is the bank on which all cheques are drawn. I believe our debt to nature is total, our willingness to pay anything back on account barely discernible. I believe that unless we recognise this debt and renegotiate it we write our own epitaph.

I believe that there is an outside chance to save the earth and most of its tenants. This outside chance must be grasped with gambler's hands.

I believe that terrible risks must be taken and terrible passions roused before these ends can hope to be accomplished. If a system is facing extreme pressures, only extreme counter-pressures are relevant, let alone likely to prove effective.

I believe that all who subscribe to these testaments must act now, stand up and be counted. What friends Nature has, Nature needs.

Books and articles mentioned in the text

Ballantyne, R. M., *The Gorilla Hunters* (1861).

Champion, F. W., *The Jungle in Sunlight and Shadow* (1933).
—, *With a Camera in Tigerland* (1934).

Crisler, Lois, *Captive Wild: nine years with wolves* (1969).

Eisenberg, McKay, Jainudeen, 'Reproductive Behaviour of the Asiatic Elephant', *Behaviour*, vol. XXXVIII (1971) pp. 3–4.

Ericson, David B., and Wollin, Goesta, *The Deep and the Past* (New York, 1964).

Ewer, R. F., *The Carnivores* (1973).
—, *Ethology of Mammals* (1968).

Fossey, Dian, 'Making Friends with Mountain Gorillas', *National Geographic Magazine*, vol. 137, no. 1 (1970) pp. 48–67.

Fremlin, J. H., 'How Many People Can the World Support?', *New Scientist*, vol. 24 (1964), pp. 285.

Goddard, J., 'Mating and Courtship of the Black Rhinoceros (*Diceros bicornis*)', *East African Wildlife Journal*, vol. 14 (1966) pp. 69–75

Goldsmith, Edward, 'Religion in a Stable Society', *Ecologist*, vol. 4, no. 9 (1974) pp. 321–5.

Goodall, Jane van Lawick, *In the Shadow of Man* (1971).

Hill, W. C. Osman, *Evolutionary Biology of the Primates* (1972).

—, *Primates: comparative anatomy and taxonomy*, 8 vols. (Edinburgh, 1953–70).

Jainudeen, Eisenberg, Tilkaratue, 'Oestrus Cycle of the Asiatic Elephant in Captivity', *Reproduction and Fertility*, vol. 27 (1971) pp. 321–8.

Kortlandt, A., 'Chimpanzees' in *Grzimek's Animal Life Encyclopaedia*, ed. B. Grzimek (1975).

Kurtèn, Björn, *The Age of Mammals* (1971).

Livingstone, David, *Missionary Travels and Researches in South Africa* (1857).

McKinnon, John, *In Search of the Red Ape* (1974).

Man and Beast: comparative social behaviour, ed. John Eisenberg and Wilton S. Dillan (Washington, D.C., 1971).

Reynolds, Vernon, *Budongo: a forest and its chimpanzees* (1965).

Schaller, George, *The Deer and the Tiger: a study of wildlife in India* (1967).

—, *The Mountain Gorilla: ecology and behaviour* (1963).

—, *The Year of the Gorilla* (1965).

Schenkel, Rudolf, 'Ecology and Behaviour of the Black Rhinoceros', *Mammalia Depicta* (Hamburg, 1969).

Zeuner, A. F. E., *A History of Domesticated Animals* (1963).

Zuckerman, Solly, *The Social Life of Monkeys and Apes* (1932).

The translation of the extract from the Norse myth of Thorolf Skallagrimsson on page 39 is by Nicholas Gould.

Illustration Acknowledgements

Harry Teyn, G.D.T.	2, 21, 24 (*below*), 34, 63 (*left*), 64, 112, 113 (*below*), 114, 116 (*below, left*), 128. Colour plates 1, 2, 5, 6, 7, 12, 13, 14, 15, 16, 17, 18.
Clive Boursnell	12, 38, 45, 94, 104, 109, 115, 116 (*above*), 136.
Crispin Eurich	30
Dmitry Kasterine	91 (*below*)
Patrick Lichfield	154
Min Murray-Threipland	Colour plates 10, 11
Kenny Parker	63 (*right*)
Bryan Wharton	141
Associated Newspapers	65, 83
Daily Mail	41, 47
Daily Mirror	6, 71, 85–88, 103
Kentish Express	54, 61
Kent Messenger	111 (*below*), 142
Keystone Press Agency	82, 92, 99, 113 (*above*), 116 (*below, right*), 147, 153
London Express	57

Where we have been unable to supply a credit at the time of going to press, we will be happy to include an appropriate acknowledgement in future printings.